TWELFTH
FAIL

Praise for *Twelfth Fail*

'Motivational and lucid! I believe this novel will inspire millions of youth to fulfil their dreams.'—**Sachin Tendulkar, cricketer**

'A novel that gives hope and strength to face any adversity.' —**K. Vijay Kumar, former advisor to the governor, Jammu and Kashmir**

'Characters in this novel sometimes remind me of those in the film *3 Idiots.'*—**Rajkumar Hirani, filmmaker**

'An amazing book that teaches determination, dedication and discipline.'—**Sunil Gavaskar, cricketer**

'An inspirational story.'—**Rajat Sharma, editor-in-chief and chairman, India TV**

'Luck smiles on those who have courage, willpower and dedication. This novel is about the wonders these qualities can accomplish.'—**Ashutosh Rana, actor**

'This book is a must read if you have the courage to dream big.' —**Ujjwal Nikam, special public prosecutor, India**

'A convincing account of human struggle—both financial and psychological.'—**Manoj Bajpayee, actor**

'This novel makes one believe nothing is impossible.'—**Anurag Kashyap, filmmaker**

'A riveting narrative.'—**O.P. Rawat, former chief election commissioner of India**

'Read this book to overcome self-doubt.'—**Dibang, journalist, ABP News**

'Even if the most depressed person goes through this novel, they will feel reinvigorated.'—**Anand Kumar, mathematician and founder, Super 30**

'A rare story of perseverance, love and passion.'—**Vishal Bhardwaj, filmmaker and music composer**

HARA VAHI JO LADA NAHI

TWELFTH FAIL

ANURAG PATHAK

TRANSLATED FROM THE HINDI ORIGINAL BY
GAUTAM CHOUBEY AND LALIT KUMAR

HarperCollins *Publishers* India

First published in India by HarperCollins *Publishers* 2021
4th Floor, Tower A, Building No. 10, Phase II, DLF Cyber City,
Gurugram, Haryana -122002
www.harpercollins.co.in

6 8 10 9 7 5

P-ISBN: 978-93-5489-442-8
E-ISBN: 978-93-5489-445-9

Twelfth Fail is based on the true story of Manoj Kumar Sharma.
Some names and identifying details have been changed to
protect the privacy of individuals.
The views and opinions expressed in this book are the author's own.
The publishers are in no way liable for the same.

Anurag Pathak asserts the moral right
to be identified as the author of this work.

Cover image: Getty Images
Cover design: Rajatveer Singh

Typeset in 10.5/13.7 Adobe Caslon Pro at
Manipal Technologies Limited, Manipal

Printed and bound at
Thomson Press (India) Ltd

MIX
Paper from
responsible sources
FSC® C010615

This book is produced from independently certified FSC® paper
to ensure responsible forest management.

Acknowledgements

I wish to thank Manoj, whose exemplary life and struggles form the very basis of this novel. Gratitude is also due to Vikas Divyakirti Sir; Sudhanshu, young film director and my friend; Sonal Didi; Sunil Chaturvedi and Shraddha. Had it not been for their unflinching support, this novel would not have seen the light of day.

Foreword

Every year, I come across thousands of young men and women, full of passion as they prepare for the civil services examinations. Some of them succeed and go on to serve the nation. But a few touch my heart, leaving a lasting impression on me. The story of two such individuals—Manoj and Shraddha—is the inspiration behind this novel.

Whenever I close my eyes and recall their story, my trust in the world grows manifold. Let people say there is a dearth of love and honesty in today's world or that fraud and deception have become quite common, but some of the incidents that I have witnessed are enough to make me believe in the goodness of the world.

I would like to share some fond memories.

One night, around twelve, my doorbell rang. It must have been September or October 2005. By then, Manoj had joined the Indian Police Service (IPS) and was undergoing training in Mussoorie. The sound of the bell startled me; all sorts of apprehensions came to my mind. However, I opened the door and found Manoj standing outside. He touched my feet, placed a Rs 500 note at my feet and said, 'Today I got my first salary. I couldn't wait to get to Delhi and share my happiness with you.' He sat for a while with me and then returned to Mussoorie to join the early morning training session. I was stunned. Hundreds of my students who become civil servants keep in touch, but never did I expect such a display of emotions. I have still preserved that note. Even demonetization couldn't flush it out of my world.

The second incident is from the period when Manoj was posted in a district of Maharashtra, having completed his training. Shraddha too had joined the Indian Revenue Service by then. One day, suddenly, I got a call from Manoj. 'Sir, my younger sister is getting married. We are unable to meet the expenses. Could you please lend me fifty-thousand rupees for a few months? I will return ten-thousand every month,' he said. I was left stunned again. I had never heard of an IPS officer, married to a lady who works for the IRS, struggle to arrange a sum so small.

I think every youth should go through this novel once—not just to discover the secret to success in the Union Public Service Commission (UPSC) exam, or to realize that it is possible even for those with awful academic records to dream of having the best job in the country, but also to know how to live life to the full, and the art of dealing with its many uncertainties. I can bet reading this story will transform you: all your negativity will melt away and your innate goodness will be strengthened. You will feel at ease with yourself, leading to a more optimistic view of life.

I have known Anurag, the author, ever since he was a student. *Twelfth Fail* is his second work, after *Revolution on WhatsApp*. In a rather short period, he has matured into a fine writer. I would like to thank him on behalf of zillions of prospective readers for presenting this narrative with such finesse; otherwise, there are many dazzling tales that remain unheard of and eventually fade away into oblivion.

New Delhi   **Vikas Divyakirti**
January 2019   Founder-director,
                                        Drishti IAS Coaching Classes

1

It was a pleasant March morning. Manoj was still asleep on the terrace. The sun had appeared on the horizon, its rays falling on his face. After dawdling for a while when he finally got up, his eyes spotted Vishnu. His friend and classmate was applying himself assiduously, no doubt to maths sums, on his own terrace. Manoj should have been doing the same; the class twelve board examinations were beginning today and mathematics was the very first paper.

Numbers and sums had never been his cup of tea, but Manoj picked up the textbook lying next to him. As he began turning the pages, he saw his chance for praise—a few women from his colony had gathered to draw water from the well in front of his house. Praise excited Manoj greatly.

He began walking up and down the terrace, reading maths questions out loud, hoping to impress the women with his diligence. He was noticed not before long. One of the women pointed towards him and said, 'My son doesn't study at all. And look at Manoj—he reads the whole night on the terrace, under the dim light of a lantern.'

His need for compliments satisfied, Manoj set the book aside and opened Gulshan Nanda's sensational novel *Ghat Ka Patthar*. Last night, he had read it till 1 a.m., but hadn't reached the climactic moment in the plot. He took ten minutes to finish the book and then went down to the well. The women were still there, filling their buckets. Seeing an old woman struggling to draw water, Manoj promptly came to her rescue and was rewarded immediately with her blessings, 'Dear son, may you pass your exam with a first division.'

Pandit Kalicharan, Vishnu's father, chose that moment to arrive with a bucket. He taught mathematics at the village school up to class eight, and knew Manoj and his abilities quite well. 'How prepared for the exam are you, Manoj?' he asked. 'Clearing the mathematics paper is not child's play. I have already warned my son that if he doesn't pass the exam with a first division, I will discontinue his studies. But,' he added, heaping praise on his own child, 'I know he is brilliant at maths; he studies with such sincerity.'

Manoj couldn't refute this claim. He took the bucket from Panditji's hands to ease his burden and walked along, praising Vishnu profusely. 'Uncle, there is no student in the entire district as bright as Vishnu. I am sure he will be the district topper this time.' As he uttered these words, a faint image of his father flashed before his eyes. It pained him and a tinge of sadness darkened his face.

2

Another day had dawned for the residents of Bilgram, a village near Joura tehsil, thirty kilometres from the district headquarters of Morena. It was a day like any other, except that a few boys and girls from the village were going to appear for the first paper of the class twelve board exams. Returning home from Panditji's house, Manoj found his mother chatting with two other women. 'Wait, I'll be there in a while,' she said, when he called to her.

But Manoj was getting late for the exam. He got ready in a hurry and was just about to step out when his mother, now squatting on the doorstep, asked in tones of deep concern, 'Wait, son, didn't Rajni make chapattis for you? You mustn't take your exam on an empty stomach.' Having passed on the responsibility of making chapattis to her fifteen-year-old daughter, Rajni, she had busied herself in chit-chat with the neighbours. Today Manoj had no appetite. He ignored his mother and, clutching a mathematics guidebook, fled without a word.

Since Bilgram was just alongside the road that connected the tehsil to the district headquarters, the villagers were quite fortunate as far as transportation went; a bus plying between Joura and Morena passed by every ten minutes. At around 9 a.m., the number of commuters gathered on the culvert began to surge. Manoj headed straight to the Hanuman statue in a small temple near the culvert and mumbled his desperate plea, 'O, Lord! Please help me sail through the maths paper. You are my only hope now.' By the time he returned to the culvert, Vishnu and his father, Pandit Kalicharan, were also there.

Seeing the father-son duo, a boy seated on the ledge of the culvert, spat out tobacco and asked playfully, 'Panditji, are you going to Joura to help Vishnu cheat in the exam?' Panditji was shepherding Vishnu to the exam centre because he wanted to ensure a safe and hassle-free journey for his son. Irked by the question, he snapped, 'You lot have neither seen a school nor read a book. What would you know about studies?' And he turned to look in the direction from which the bus was to come.

But no one conceded defeat so easily in this village. The insult hurled by Panditji had rattled all the boys who sat around. One of them asked nastily, 'What good are studies? Does one become a thanedar? One only gets to be a teacher in a school like the one over there and spends a lifetime telling students to repeat tables.'

To stop the situation from getting out of hand, Manoj stepped in saying, 'Teaching is such a prestigious profession. If I ever land such a job, I'll be thrilled.'

'But one has to pass class twelve for that,' taunted another boy. 'How will you pull that off, Manoj? Besides, there are rumours this year that the SDM (sub-divisional magistrate) will crack down on cheating.'

This was a worrying new information. Never had Manoj thought of hearing something so unsettling just before an exam. He comforted himself with the thought that cheating, a time-honoured practice at Vidysagar Higher Secondary School in Joura, could not be stopped so abruptly. Cheating would help him pass these board exams, much as he had cheated his way to success in the tenth board.

A tempo paused on the culvert, making a *dhad-dhad* sound. The ear-splitting racket disrupted Manoj's chain of thought. The vehicle was being driven by his friend, Balle. Manoj got on, as did Vishnu and Pandit Kalicharan. Moments later, a fifty-two-seater bus belonging to Balaji Bus Services parked right behind the tempo. Even though the bus was already chock-a-block with some seventy passengers, its skinny twenty-year-old conductor was annoyed to see Balle whisking away three passengers. 'Hey, you,' he yelled. 'How many more passengers will you take? You already have three extra; ask them to get down. They are mine.'

Bus operators had become touchy over the last few months because three or four tempos had started plying this route and eaten into their profits.

'Mind your own business,' snapped Balle. 'This is my village!' He then added menacingly, like a lion in its own territory, 'And your bus can't ply on our roads.'

Balaji Bus Services was owned by a powerful man, rich and politically well-connected. The regional transport officer (RTO) and the local police thanedar, in return for steady monetary gains, had extended their loyal protection to him. The bus staff therefore routinely broke the law, confident in their special rights to take on more passengers than legally allowed.

As Balle and the opposing party continued to exchange compliments, the dispute escalated and villagers began gathering alongside the tempo as this was a suitable occasion to put the unity of the village on display. Seeing the enemy's side grow in strength, the middle-aged driver signalled the conductor to withdraw. His many years on the job had taught him that running was the best strategy when trapped alone in a hostile village. Later, one should try to drag the conflict into one's own territory.

The conductor retreated to the bus grumbling in frustration, but not before warning Balle, who was presently swinging from the tempo's door, of unpleasant consequences. 'We will make you forget all about driving a tempo on the road, you watch out!' he yelled.

No less a strongman, Balle yelled back, 'Your bus will never pass through this village, keep that in mind.' And then he started his tempo, put it into top gear, and sped off towards Joura. As soon as they arrived at the school's gate, Manoj and Vishnu got off and walked in, while Pandit Kalicharan left for a relative's house, satisfied that his son had reached the examination centre safely.

Narendra Singh, the manager of the school, had worked really hard to get his institution recognized as one of the centres for the senior secondary board examination. He had also already promised the examinees, quite openly, that his school would support cheating and other malpractices. Historically speaking, students of the region were known to flunk mathematics, English and science papers. The prospect of cheating had drawn many to the school—more than its allotted quota of students. That day, hordes of students could be seen entering the campus, brimming with fear, but also with wonder and exhilaration at the chance of cheating their way to success. Standing by the window of his room, Narendra Singh marvelled at the sight, his gaze raining benedictions on the incoming crowd.

Today it would be the school's senior mathematics teacher, Dubeyji's, turn to ensure the smooth execution of cheating. Since it would be inconvenient for him to visit every classroom in the building, a large shamiana had been set up on the school grounds, bringing all the examinees under its welcome roof. Wooden planks had been provided for the students to sit on comfortably and write their paper. The bell rang, and question papers were handed out. Manoj looked at his paper casually once or twice, and decided to wait for Dubeyji to act.

Dubeyji was in his office, trying to solve the questions. The assignment required both labour and expertise. Once a question was solved, he had to get the complete solution written on the blackboard in the shamiana, before tackling the next question. Just as the very first solution was being copied out on the blackboard, a hubbub could be heard at the school gate. A white Bolero, with a flashing yellow beacon light, had entered the premises. In no time, five uniformed police constables invaded the shamiana.

Dubeyji saw the police and his first reaction was to panic, until he remembered that this inspection was an empty formality routinely carried out each year by the local administration on the first day of the board examinations. What was there to be afraid of? Unfortunately, the policemen were busy snatching notes and guidebooks and shoving them into sacks. Gripped by fresh anxiety, Dubeyji lit a bidi, hurriedly rubbed the blackboard clean with a duster, and dashed to Manager Narendra Singh's office seeking refuge.

The examinees, on the other hand, were still confident that the police would leave after a ten-minute drill, and the supply of answers would resume shortly. Holding on to this faith, they managed to maintain their composure. After ten minutes, notes and guidebooks were still being taken away, and then they began to get worried. The threat of failure loomed large. 'That is SDM Dushyant Singh,' said a boy, pointing to the sub-divisional magistrate, now playing the lead role in the day's drama and scolding Narendra Singh.

'You ought to be ashamed of yourself,' the SDM was saying, 'encouraging malpractices openly.' The students were now scared; the situation looked serious. But Manoj was more surprised than scared when he saw the power a government officer could display. The SDM's swagger was awe-inspiring. Even Inspector Kushwaha of Joura police post, known for his overbearing ways, looked subdued and stood meekly in front of the SDM—a man half his age. Realizing that cheating would not take place at least today, the students began cursing the SDM.

Narendra Singh—unable to understand how his arrangements, so wonderfully put in place to make cheating easier, were now being shred to pieces by the SDM—rang up the joint director of school education in desperation. That officer was familiar with Dushyant Singh's style of working, 'Nothing can be done about him,' he replied. 'Officers like him take pleasure in destroying well-established systems.' He added seriously that bad times had fallen upon Joura.

The shamiana now looked deserted as the students had left, leaving behind blank answer sheets. Only Manoj had not abandoned his copy. He had heard somewhere that it was possible to pass an examination by simply filling up the answer sheet. Based on this wisdom, he decided not to leave any page blank, and filled each page with the questions copied over and over again. In between, he kept writing 'hence proved'.

The evaluator might even simply look at the 'hence proved', thought Manoj, and consider the question solved. On the last page of the script, he wrote a moving plea: 'I could not concentrate on my studies because my grandmother was extremely unwell. I will be forever indebted to the examiner if I pass the examination.'

3

One morning, while Manoj's result was still awaited, several cricket-mad boys from the village gathered at Balle's doorstep. Manoj was counted among the better players of the team (not for any ability to hit the ball hard, but for his fielding skills). Also in a crisis, when wickets fell in quick succession, Manoj could be relied upon to rescue the team by standing firm on the crease.

'Today, there is a tournament in Joura,' announced Balle. 'The entry fee is a hundred rupees and a cricket ball will cost us another ten, so each of us will have to put in ten rupees.'

Manoj knew that arranging the money wasn't going to be easy. In October, seven months ago, his father had returned from Dindori and handed Rs 10,000 to his mother. Seven months later, there was nothing left. His father had neither returned, nor sent anything more, and his mother was compelled to borrow from neighbours to meet daily expenses. The family lived in the hope that one day he would return and all their troubles would vanish.

The upcoming tournament in Joura only brought the sad image of his ramshackle house to Manoj's eyes. He went home to find his mother gossiping with a neighbourhood aunty—the two standing at the latter's door. Kamlesh, his younger brother, wasn't home. As always, he would either be loafing by the culvert, or would have gone to Joura without informing anyone. Being an aimless loafer was his only hobby.

His mother's tittle-tattle finally came to an end and she had no choice but to head home. Manoj promptly cornered her and asked, 'Mummy, can you spare ten rupees for a cricket match?'

Visibly upset, she replied, 'I have no money! Your father hasn't shown up in seven months; I have been borrowing to meet the household expenses!'

Manoj had known his chances were bleak. So he ignored his disappointment, put on his muddied white canvas shoes, and ran to join his teammates.

The tournament had been organized at Joura's Mandi Maidan. Inside a shamiana sat fifty plastic chairs—for players of both teams, the commentators, and the chief guest. Since Manoj was the only one who hadn't paid his share in the twelve-member team, he wouldn't get to play. Sadly, he went in and quietly sat on a chair. Pappu Singh, the lead singer of Joura's Dayal Band, in charge of the running commentary, was already there.

'Hello, mike-testing, hello. The match is about to start and fans are requested to settle down. You there, red shirt, do not walk over the pitch. Black shirt, I see a cow entering the ground. Chase it out.' Commentary had commenced from the scene of action. 'Today's chief guest, our SDM Sahib, is caught up with some work; he'll join us later,' the commentator informed the crowd.

It was a match with ten overs. Bilgram won the toss and decided to bowl first. The opposition batted fiercely, making a total of 112 runs. Balle and Prakash opened the innings for Bilgram. No sooner had Balle dispatched the first two balls to the boundary, a buzz of excitement ran through the shamiana. Commentator Pappu Singh was ecstatic, 'Stop the game! Chief guest SDM Sahib is here.'

The SDM graciously signalled that the match be continued. However, Pappu Singh persisted with his commentary, instructing the organizers to welcome the guest. 'Devendra Agarwal is requested to garland SDM Sahib,' he blared.

Although Dushyant Singh protested, Devendra Agarwal ensured that the garland brought specially for the occasion made it around the guest's neck.

'Arrey, Bhai,' protested the SDM, 'all this isn't necessary; it disturbs the flow of the game. Let the match continue.' He looked serious about the tournament.

Manoj got a chance to observe him from close proximity. The SDM's raid to thwart cheating had harmed Manoj, but he was large-hearted enough to be impressed by the SDM's fearless spirit and now stood up to say namaste. The chief guest reciprocated with a smile. The game resumed and an excited Pappu Singh linked the match to patriotic sentiments by crooning an old Mohammed Rafi song about a dying soldier urging his comrades to fight on:

Kar chale hum fida jaan-o-tan sathiyon,
Ab tumhare hawale watan sathiyon

Dushyant Singh found melody in the middle of a match quite distracting. He turned to Pappu Singh and said bluntly, 'Must you sing? Focus on commentary.'

Pappu Singh obeyed. 'Bilgram has lost two wickets. A buffalo must have barged into their farm; those two seemed to be in such a hurry.' The two-penny commentary irritated Dushyant Singh even more, and annoyance was writ large on his face.

By the seventh over, Bilgram had lost five wickets and had made fifty-five runs. Balle stood solid on forty, even as wickets kept tumbling at the other end. Manoj knew had he been in the middle-order batting, he would have protected his wicket and his team could have won. Alas, for the want of just ten rupees, the team was about to lose the match. Even as he was struggling with his frustration, Pappu Singh entrusted him with the mike and rushed away to relieve himself of a long-suppressed urge to pee.

Manoj used the opportunity to speak his heart: 'The team from Bilgram is in a spot of bother. Skipper Balle's poor strategy has cost them dearly. In spite of his brilliant innings, wickets are falling at the other end. They desperately need a batsman who can stand solid. Sadly, the team seems to lack such a hero.' Pointless jokes had given way to serious analysis; the mood of commentary had changed dramatically.

Dushyant Singh took note of the difference and looked impressed. When Pappu Singh returned to reclaim the mike, Dushyant Singh ordered him to let Manoj continue with the commentary. 'Let the boy speak. And you sit clear of him.'

His hurt at not being able to play thus alleviated by the SDM's unexpected praise, Manoj carried on with great enthusiasm till the end of the game. Soon, the last wicket fell and it was all over for the Bilgram team. Balle and the other players returned to the shamiana, heads bowed in disappointment. Manoj's commentary took a poetic turn to express his feelings and he said, 'A boat that fears the crashing waves never sails across the ocean, but those who persist are never defeated. Therefore, today's match will be remembered for Balle's heroic efforts. In spite of the loss, he deserves huge applause.'

Manoj had deftly shifted the focus from Bilgram's loss to Balle's valiant batting. The losing team's pride was intact, all thanks to his commentary. Once the certificates were distributed, the SDM turned to Manoj and said, 'Bravo! You speak so well. What is your name?'

'Manoj Kumar Sharma.'

The team from Bilgram hopped into Balle's tempo and set off for their village. That day, Dushyant Singh had heaped praise on a boy who wanted to win praise all the time. Naturally, Manoj's heart was bursting with joy.

4

It had been a month since Ranveer Sharma, Manoj's father, had come back home. His mother had finally received all the suspended instalments of his father's salary. Debts were paid off. But there was something fishy about his protracted stay. Manoj's mother knew her husband too well. He would stay away at work for months on end, least bothered about his household. Now after a month-long holiday, he was showing zero inclination to return. As an officer employed by the agricultural department of the state government, was he entitled to such long leave?

One day, his mother had enough and asked him at the top of her voice, 'When do you plan to return to work?'

Manoj's father, who hated people interfering with his professional life, yelled back, 'Mind your own business! What do you know about jobs? Has anyone in your family ever been employed? Rustic! Illiterate!'

'Yes, no one from my family has ever held a job,' retorted his mother. 'But I don't understand how you manage to keep yours. When you disappear for months at a stretch, in whose care do you leave your family?'

His father was a tough cookie, not to be rattled. He ignored her and returned to his perusal of some official documents. At this point, his father's brother, Shyamsundar, came running up the stairs, sat on the bed and announced, 'Bhaisahib, Manoj has failed.'

One would have expected Bhaisahib to be either enraged or grief-stricken at the news. However, he remained unfazed. He collected the scattered papers around him, deposited them in the box underneath the bed, and prepared to leave. Seeing his brother coolly walk away, Shyamsundar spiced up the news and made another bid to provoke him, 'Except Hindi, the boy has failed in every subject.'

Manoj's father remained unfazed; it was as though the news concerned a stranger and not his son. His face, bereft of any expression—no pleasure, no pain, anger or humiliation—expressed an immunity to petty things like success–failure, fame–infamy, progress–regress, profit–loss and so forth. He ignored Shyamsundar, locked the box with a pint-sized lock, tugged at it once or twice to ensure it wouldn't give way, pushed the box under the bed and sat down again.

Perhaps Shyamsundar desired a longish chat on a matter as interesting as Manoj's failure, because he tried again. 'In physics, mathematics and chemistry, he couldn't even touch double digits. In English, he has scored twelve out of fifty.' But the iron-hearted father managed to ignore his son's progress report.

Shocked at the indifference on display, Manoj's mother broke her silence and chided him, 'The boy has failed and he is least bothered.'

The father simply lit a cigarette and settled more comfortably on the bed. He pulled hard on the cigarette and looked up at Shyamsundar. Determined to remind his elder brother of his responsibilities, Shyamsundar said, 'I had already asked you to take Manoj along. Under your strict supervision, he may have shown a little interest in studies. Staying in the village, he was sure to become a loafer. As expected, he has failed.'

Manoj had lived with his father till class eight. For some years—at Raipur, Gariaband and later Farsabad—the entire family lived together. However, since the last four years, Manoj, along with his mother, his brother, Kamlesh and their younger sister, Rajni, had been forced to live in the village. His father had refused to take them along to Dindori. These four years—the most decisive ones of Manoj's academic life—got wasted in the village. Kamlesh, who had no love for studies, had quit after class eight. And since Rajni was a girl, their father felt no need to fret over her education. Naturally, he did not share Shyamsundar's enthusiasm for the discussion.

Sitting comfortably on the bed, he flicked ash off the burnt end of his cigarette and in his hoarse voice concluded with a pithy observation. 'He'll pass the next year,' he said, and went down the stairs, his gait carefree. On the way down, he hurled a snide remark at Manoj's mother. 'It's ten already. When will you make breakfast? Do you plan to starve me to death?'

When Manoj learnt that he had failed in every subject except Hindi, he went to the Hanuman temple near the culvert and wept for a very long time. He had scored sixty-two in Hindi; it was not only the easiest of papers, but it was his favourite. He loved reading novels, poems and stories. However, Hindi alone could not see him through. He was disappointed with English; like the other papers, it too had ditched him. While writing an essay on the subject 'My Best Friend', he could only get the first sentence—Rakesh is my best friend—correct. The rest of it, which comprised no more than two or three lines, was full of spelling and grammatical errors.

Having wept to his heart's content, he stepped out of the temple and went to meet Rakesh, who consoled him and said, 'You've spent an entire day lamenting; for how much longer do you intend to look sullen?'

Vishnu had passed with a first division. While he was thrilled at his own performance, he too felt obligated to console his friend. 'I always asked you to focus on studies. One can't rely on cheating.'

'Mathematic beats me. How am I supposed to study?' Manoj retorted.

Absorbed in their chit-chat, the three friends reached the well near Manoj's house. A few women were busy fetching water. 'Lalla, there you are! Help me with the bucket,' an old woman said to Manoj. Customary aid elicited a customary blessing: 'Lalla, may you pass with a first division.'

Manoj reacted with a weak smile. Shyamsundar, standing nearby, overheard the exchange and couldn't help sticking his nose in. 'Dear Tai,' he said to the old woman loudly, to ensure everyone around heard, 'forget about a first division, Manoj has failed.'

Manoj was hurt by this public humiliation. 'What good is studying any more?' said Rakesh, blurting out the thought stuck in his head for some time. 'Those with BAs and MAs wear out their shoes looking for work. I'm telling you, you should start a business.' Manoj liked the idea, but he was also aware of his family's financial condition. 'One needs about a lakh to start a business. Where will the money come from?'

He went home, hopeless and full of doubts about his future. His younger brother, Kamlesh, had been missing since morning. Mother was quite worried. When she shared her concerns with her husband, reassurance was forthcoming, 'Don't worry, he'll be back by the morning. You should rather focus on getting dinner ready.' And then he left to stroll on the terrace, without a care in the world.

The following morning, Kamlesh returned. He had spent the night at a friend's place in Joura.

5

Kamlesh had not returned empty-handed from Joura, he had brought home a bright idea—a brand-new plan to restore the family's fortunes. And this he explained to his father at length. 'Balle is buying a new tempo and so he's selling the old one for forty thousand. One can easily make eight to ten thousand per month. I'll drive it.'

Manoj found Kamlesh's scheme quite practical. He knew fully well that as a twelfth fail he would never get a government job; it was time for him too to think of a livelihood. Besides, most boys in the village were engaged in professions that generated a similar income. Some drove tempos, others worked as electricians. Those with a little money had opened grocery shops in Joura. Many ran STD booths, which were in vogue then. And the few with sufficient farmland, farmed. Manoj's father and uncle together had only three bigha land—barely enough to produce a year's supply of wheat for the family—so that option was ruled out. Manoj felt he had no choice but to start a business.

His father, who had no money to put into buying a tempo, chose to berate his son on other grounds. 'Do you plan to ruin the family's name by working as an auto driver? Don't you realize ours is a well-educated family?'

The son was silenced, but not the mother. 'Wah!' she said. 'Such a reputed family! What happens to your reputation when I go around borrowing? The boys want to work hard and achieve something in life. But look at yourself—instead of helping them, you're creating hurdles.'

The mother's complaint forced the father into a yogic silence.

The next morning, when she went upstairs to Manoj's father's room, he was putting his clothes into a bag. She had gone up to persuade him to buy the tempo. But the man, who had camped at home for over a month, negligent of his job, was suddenly ready to leave. 'There is a lot of work pending in the office. I should return now. Hurry, get the food ready. I'll eat before leaving.'

Mother was livid, but didn't want to say anything harsh; it would have been inauspicious since he was to embark on a journey.

His sudden departure put a temporary hold on the tempo scheme. However, the next morning, Kamlesh stubbornly repeated his demand. 'Well, your father ran away in the nick of time,' retorted his mother. 'What do you expect from me? Where am I supposed to get forty-thousand rupees from?'

After a long discussion, a plan was devised. 'I have ten thousand on me. We will borrow another thirty thousand from Pandit Kalicharan. There is a little jewellery in the house; we'll mortgage it,' his mother declared.

And so Balle's second-hand tempo was bought for Rs 40,000. The entire family was brimming over with hope and confidence. Kamlesh settled on the driver's seat and conductor Manoj was put in charge of collecting fares from passengers. It was their first day at work. Manoj started calling out: 'Chaira, Bharra, Bagcheeni, Morena.' Soon, the tempo set out for its maiden trip to Morena with five passengers on board.

The business seemed promising. Back from work at night, Manoj handed over Rs 200—the first day's earnings—to his mother. The gesture overwhelmed her; her sons had started earning. The day-long toil showed on Manoj. His hair was dusty, his clothes soiled and his lips parched. Seeing her son look so pitiable, his mother was moved to tears. Manoj hugged her and said, 'What's to worry? Your sons have started earning now.'

This went on for a month. Each evening, the sons would hand over their daily earnings, about Rs 200, to the mother. At this rate, she felt the debt would soon be paid off. And then, in a year or two, they could get a new tempo. Her husband's neglect had forced her to turn to her sons; their labour, she hoped, would put the house back in order.

Things were going well, until the day the tempo reached the Bagchini crossing while a police inspection was in progress. The constable waved Manoj to a stop. 'What's the matter, Divanji?' he asked, getting down. 'Why did you stop us? We have all the documents.' He produced the driving license and registration papers.

'Thanedar's orders. Go ask him,' the constable replied, getting into their tempo and driving it to the police station 200 metres down the road.

Manoj and Kamlesh had no choice but to run after their vehicle. Just then, the Balaji Bus Service vehicle whizzed past them. Its conductor stuck his head out and shouted, 'What's up? Didn't I say I'd make you forget all about plying a tempo? Go, try now.'

He was the same conductor who had fought Balle earlier. He had recognized the tempo. When Manoj heard his words, he understood that they had fallen victim to the bus operator's conspiracy.

The thanedar was a seasoned policeman of fifty-five. 'Sir, all our papers are in order,' pleaded Manoj, full of fear, 'but my tempo has been confiscated.'

The thanedar ignored him and addressed the constable instead, 'Divanji, bring the man who's waiting outside.' Divanji obeyed and soon returned with a twenty-year-old youth. The young man was a small-time thief and also a police informant. His name was Dinesh. 'Tell me, Dinesh, what's your complaint?' asked the thanedar.

Dinesh was ready with his well-rehearsed story. 'My friend and I were out on a cycle. His tempo dashed into us. My friend fell and fainted; I had to get him admitted at the primary health centre. I'm coming straight from there.'

The thanedar turned to Manoj and asked, 'Got it? You cause a road accident and yet have the nerve to argue with me?'

Manoj choked up. 'This man is lying. We haven't been involved in any accident.'

'Quiet! You bastard!' shouted the thanedar, showing his true colours. 'Lock them up,' he ordered. 'When they rot in jail, they'll remember all about the accident.'

In return for a 'fee' paid by the Balaji Bus Services owner, the thanedar had completed his assignment to perfection. Manoj and Kamlesh were in utter shock and started crying, but the thanedar remained unmoved. The constable pushed them behind bars and locked the door. The brothers cried themselves sick. Shaking with fear, they didn't know whom to ask for help.

About two hours later, the constable said, 'You should be thankful that we aren't keeping you here for the night. Thanedar Sahib is a kind-hearted man. You may go now. But you'll have to go to court to claim your vehicle.'

There were many tempos parked outside the police station, all rusting away in the hope that one day the court would set them free. The brothers knew what this meant for their tempo—it was destined to meet the same fate.

Once out of the police station, they ran for their lives. This was their first brush with the law. For them, the police station was a ravisher, not a protector. As it was already night, there were no buses or tempos plying. They walked 10 kilometres home—dejected, sad, broken, defeated and teary-eyed. As soon as Manoj saw his mother, he broke down. When she heard the details, she too started crying. Their great hope of ridding the family of its troubles—a hope that was gradually building up—had suddenly come crashing down. But she steeled her heart and consoled Manoj, 'Don't worry, everything will be okay.'

The whole night Manoj lay awake on the terrace. Sleep had deserted him.

6

The long night was over, and a new morning had dawned. Tears of desperation had dried up. The great dream that had inspired their new venture was over. For the past one month, efforts had been made to strengthen a financially fragile family. These attempts were now abandoned.

Manoj needed a friend to lean on, someone who could stop the storm raging inside his heart. His feet took him to Rakesh's house, where he raged without stopping to explain, 'Those who work hard to earn an honest living are put in prison. The police behave as though we are thieves or dacoits. Those with a fleet of buses and money in their pockets, do they own the road? Does a poor man have no right to ply his tempo?'

When he ran out of steam, he narrated the entire ordeal. Rakesh, trying to lessen his pain, explained, 'It happened to you, so you are all worked up, but this is an everyday struggle for survival where the poor get grounded and pounded. It's no big a deal. Everyone knows about this.'

'But it is so unfair!' Manoj was seething. 'Why are those who work hard and honestly made to suffer?'

Rakesh imparted further practical wisdom as bluntly as possible. 'This is why people work hard, educate their children, and get friendly with politicians and policemen. If only you had money, you would've slapped the thanedar with it. Had you been close to a politician, an MLA, a collector, or a police superintendent, they would have put in a word for you. But you are a pauper—a *than-than* Gopal. No important person knows you, nor are you friends with anyone powerful.'

'What do you mean to say?' demanded Manoj. 'Shouldn't the police ensure that the poor aren't charged with false cases and tortured?'

In response, Rakesh could only ram home the ugly truth. 'Men fight over passengers and it often gets bloody. Weren't bullets fired near Joura culvert last month? Did one not hit a tempo driver in his thigh? You have to let it go. People like you should not be in the transport business. These quarrels, arrests, court cases and daily fights on the street, I bet you can't handle any of these.'

The incident that had shaken Manoj so deeply had been dismissed by Rakesh as quite common. Yet, whenever the thanedar's face came to mind, Manoj felt the rage grow in his heart. 'I can't forget the thanedar,' he said.

Rakesh was equally firm. 'So be it! But all thanedars are quite alike; they aren't apostles of truth like Raja Harishchandra.'

'There must be good ones too,' thought Manoj in desperation, 'who do the right things and don't frame people falsely; those who uphold the law.' His agony searched for a ray of hope in that engulfing darkness—an assurance that law and justice were still alive. But Rakesh simply said, 'I have never known a good thanedar.'

Then he added slowly, 'I heard that the SDM Dushyant Singh helps the poor. He works honestly. People praise him a lot. You should meet him. Perhaps he can help you with the tempo?'

Manoj liked the suggestion. It gave him a glimmer of hope.

7

Amidst the surging crowd at Joura's tehsil office were Manoj and Kamlesh, hoping to meet Dushyant Singh and get back their tempo. Manoj wasn't sure how to approach him; hesitation weakened his courage. Dushyant Singh had praised his commentary and called him talented. Were he to approach him for the tempo, the truth about his life would come out.

Even as he was brooding over the matter, weighing his options, the doorman put a requisition slip into his hands. He had to fill in his name and the reason he wanted to meet the SDM. He wrote his name, but could not bring himself to write 'to get my tempo released' in the 'Reason' column. He somehow feared that writing it so bluntly would ruin his chances of meeting the SDM. Besides, he wanted Dushyant Singh to remember him as the talented fellow. Racking his brains, he finally came up with an ingenious reason: 'to discuss career and studies'. With that sent, he hoped Dushyant Singh would consider him a bright student and speak to him warmly. During the conversation, he'd find a chance to mention his tempo.

As he stood at the gate juggling his thoughts, he was summoned. The SDM had called for him.

Dushyant Singh was seated behind a large table. His reader was laying the case files out on the table. When he saw Manoj, he turned to his reader and said, 'This is Manoj, Joura's best commentator. He'll cover the match between the administration and lawyers next Sunday.'

Manoj hadn't hoped for such respect. He felt proud of himself. Kamlesh too couldn't conceal his joy, and whispered, 'I have a feeling we're getting our tempo back. This SDM knows you well.'

Manoj gestured to him to stay quiet just as Dushyant Singh spoke again. 'This is the first time someone has come to me without any official work. Otherwise, people only approach me for firearm licenses or to get gamblers and betters released from jail,' he said with a laugh and started examining the files in front of him.

'Sir, this is from Bagcheeni. The case is about disturbing the peace,' said the reader, pointing to the next file.

Inspector Yadav of Bagcheeni Police Station had arrested a forty-year-old man on charges of causing a ruckus. The accused, having already spent a day in jail, had been brought to the SDM's court for further legal action. The SDM had to decide whether the apprehended was guilty as charged. The brothers noticed how Yadav saluted the SDM and kept standing attentively; he lacked the courage to occupy a chair in the SDM's presence. He was the man who had confiscated their tempo, the very same thanedar against whom they had a complaint.

'Tell me, Inspector Sahib, what's the matter?' said the SDM.

'Sir, yesterday the accused, Mukesh, fired two shots from a country-made pistol near his neighbour Naresh's house. The police wants Mukesh to be jailed for causing disturbance in his locality.'

'Do you have a witness?' the SDM wanted to know.

'Yes, sir.' And he called the witness.

The brothers were stunned to see the witness. 'Isn't this Dinesh, the man who has framed us?' Kamlesh whispered to his brother. 'I see it quite clearly now. He is thanedar's pet dog; a professional liar. That means this case is false too. Poor Mukesh! He is trapped. The thanedar won't rest till Mukesh is jailed.'

For a moment, Manoj felt a strong urge to share everything with the SDM. He wanted to tell him that the witness was a fraud and a crook, that getting innocent people framed was his profession, that the thanedar too was dishonest and corrupt, that he often charged people with false cases. But he couldn't gather the necessary courage. The proceedings went on. 'Mukesh, do you wish to say something in your defence, or shall I send you to a jail?' asked the SDM.

At this, the inspector's face lit up with joy; Mukesh, by contrast, shook with fear. He joined his hands in supplication and pleaded, 'Sir, I have committed no crime. You may ask my wife and daughter.' A woman and a girl of seventeen or eighteen were brought into the room.

'Huzoor,' said the woman between sobs, 'he is completely innocent. It is all Naresh's mischief. He had sworn to get him jailed. About a year ago, he had borrowed ten-thousand rupees from us, which he didn't return, in spite of repeated reminders. Now, he has dragged us to the police.' She sobbed even louder at this.

Manoj saw his own lawsuit mirrored in Mukesh's ordeal—a trap with all exists blocked by the inspector. Dushyant Singh heard the woman out and resumed witness examination. 'Witness Dinesh, move forward; I can't see your face properly.'

Dinesh straightened up, arched his neck like an ostrich, but wouldn't make eye contact with the SDM. 'Look up, and answer,' said the SDM sternly. 'How many houses do you burgle every month?'

Dinesh began to sweat. The inspector—till then without a worry—began to feel a bit uneasy.

Manoj was baffled. How could the SDM know the truth about Dinesh with just a glimpse at him? The SDM's sharp intellect and his ability to read a person surprised him.

The SDM pointed to Mukesh and asked Dinesh, 'Where did he fire?'

'Sir, at Naresh's house,' answered Dinesh.

'Was Naresh known to you before the incident?'

'No, huzoor.'

'Then how did you know it was Naresh's house?'

Rattled by the question, Dinesh looked to the inspector for a cue. But the inspector had nothing to say either. Dinesh was hopelessly trapped. Mukesh's truth was poised for victory while the corrupt inspector's conspiracy was on the verge of certain defeat. Dushyant Singh turned to the inspector and said, 'Yadavji, this is a false case and is framed by you; you know this as well as I do. Your witness hadn't seen anything. He is lying.'

Manoj wanted to rise to his feet and clap. Today, he had seen an honest man bring a corrupt system to account. Ever since his tempo was confiscated, the plight of the poor and the helpless had haunted him.

Thereafter, the SDM dictated his order: 'The case stands dismissed. Since Mukesh has not committed any crime, he is to be released. The police department is hereby instructed to file a case against Dinesh for deposing falsely. Further, the police department is also instructed to initiate an inquiry against Inspector Yadav for fabricating a case.' So saying, he signed the order letter before dumping the file on his reader's table.

Manoj was delighted; he could not believe that a man could sift the truth from a lie in such a short time, that a scoundrel could be punished so swiftly, that an honest man could get

instant justice. Lost in a trance—a world of ecstasy and wonder—
he forgot all about his tempo.

'So, Manoj, you want to talk about your career,' said Dushyant
Singh. He had not forgotten the reason behind Manoj's visit.

'Yes, sir,' replied Manoj, as though waking up from a dream.

'What is your aim? What do you want to be?'

'Sir, I want to be like you,' blurted out Manoj, totally
enchanted by the SDM's charisma. But the twelfth fail did not
know the way forward. He was simply smitten by the position
and the power it commanded.

'Excellent,' replied the SDM. 'We must always have high
goals; nothing is impossible if a man is determined. In which
class do you study?'

The SDM's encouraging words had led Manoj on to a
dream-filled path, but the question dragged him back to thorny
reality. 'Sir, I have recently passed class twelve,' he lied to his idol.
He was afraid that if he told the truth about his failure and about
the confiscated tempo, the SDM would not entertain him. He
wanted to erase his below-ordinary life through lies.

'Manoj, to work for the state services, you will have to
first clear the Madhya Pradesh Public Services Commission
examination called PSC; those selected become a sub-divisional
magistrate, an SDM. The SDM is deployed in a sub-division.'
Dushyant Singh simplified everything for Manoj.

'Sir, how does one pass the exam?' asked Manoj. He was
moving up a road that had hitherto only held mysteries.

'You'll have to pass two subjects of your choice,' said the
SDM. 'Besides, there is a compulsory paper that tests your
general knowledge too.' Manoj was relieved to learn that
mathematics and English did not play a big part in the exam.
Dushyant Singh told him that even though he had a degree in
mechanical engineering, he chose Hindi literature and history

as his papers in the PSC exam. He also shared the strategy to clear the exam.

The SDM had entrusted twelfth-fail Manoj with a dream; it looked distant and hazy, yet promising. With that lodged deep in his heart, he returned home. Not once did he request the SDM to get his tempo released. Naturally, Kamlesh was livid and abused Manoj all the way back home.

8

A visibly enthused Manoj reached Rakesh's house and found Vishnu already there. 'Rakesh,' Manoj announced, 'I wish to become an SDM, just like Dushyant Sir.'

'I am sure you will,' said Rakesh, collecting buffalo dung in a basket. 'It isn't such a big deal. They do not come down from the sky. Those who become SDMs are also mortals like us.'

Vishnu had dissolved into laughter at twelfth-fail Manoj making such grand plans and now clapped hysterically, still laughing. Once he calmed down a bit, he told Manoj not to be a braggart. 'Forget about becoming a deputy collector; it's a tall ask anyway. You aren't good enough for even a clerical job. A twelfth fail wants to be an SDM! Huh! A man shouldn't dream beyond his means.'

This truth crushed the seeds of ambition beginning to take root in Manoj's heart; the ridicule shattered his dream. A twelfth fail had no right to nurture such high goals. He sat down dismayed, his head drooping. But Rakesh was not convinced. 'I still hold that if a man perseveres, he can become whoever he wants to be,' he said, scooping up a second pile of dung.

Vishnu turned to him with scorn. 'What do you know about studies? Focus on the dung in your basket. When someone like me with a first division in class twelve, doesn't have the nerve to think of becoming a deputy collector, can a twelfth fail achieve this feat? Out of the millions who sit for the exam, barely fifteen or twenty candidates make it through.'

The faint glimmer of hope that had briefly shone after the reassurance from Rakesh suddenly disappeared. Thanks to Vishnu, the storm that raged in Manoj's head now abated. Meanwhile, Rakesh was humbly admitting he was no scholar. 'I am an illiterate simpleton in the habit of blurting out whatever comes to my mind. Please don't feel offended, Vishnu.'

Pleased at his triumph, Vishnu turned to counsel Manoj. 'You can't clear class twelve, not in this life. So take my advice. Our village lacks a decent eatery and there is a great demand for samosas, mangode and jalebis. It's more profitable to fry mangode than to drive a tempo. Spend some time training under Babulal Mangodewallah of Joura, and then start your own shop in the village.'

Rakesh's buffaloes, having gone out to graze in the fields, were now returning having eaten their fill. A little calf had followed its mother too, prancing its way back home. When Rakesh saw Vishnu getting a little carried away and the tension ratcheting up, he tried to distract him. 'You worry too much, Vishnu. Listen, will you please do something for me? Tether Roopa to the peg. Meanwhile, I'll water the calf.'

Content with the outcome of the debate, Vishnu readily acceded to the request. The buffalo, however, was not so happy. Accustomed to being shepherded by Rakesh, it got agitated, shook its neck violently and charged. In his hurry to get away, Vishnu fell on his back. Rakesh quickly intervened and the cause of all the commotion was quietly led away by him. Stunned by the assault, Vishnu was breathing rapidly. As soon as he composed himself, he berated Rakesh.

Rakesh smiled and told him, 'In the beginning, Roopa used to charge at me too; she even knocked me over once or twice. But gradually, as she started recognizing me, her aggression disappeared. And now, she's become really smart. She goes out alone to graze in the distant fields, and returns home all by herself.' And he caressed Roopa's neck, who responded to the touch of affection by shaking her head.

'Look here, Vishnu, thanks to daily practice, this buffalo has memorized the route back home. If animals can learn a trick by repetition, can't we humans too? Nothing is impossible for a man. Only practice makes one perfect.' Using a proverb he had learnt as a child, Rakesh had said it all.

An illiterate philosophizing about success, that too using his buffalo as an example, was beyond Vishnu's expectations; it took him by surprise. And once again, a spark of hope dispelled the thick blanket of darkness that had enveloped Manoj's mind.

9

It was June, hot and humid.

Manoj was on the road to Gwalior, escorted by his uncle Moolchand, a bag dangling from his hands. Walking under a scorching afternoon sun, he was drenched to the bones with sweat. But his heart was buoyant with hope. At last, they reached their destination—Triloki's room. Triloki was Moolchand's brother-in-law. 'Triloki,' he said, 'Manoj will pursue BA at MLB College. Please see to it that he gets admission.'

Triloki, a second-year student at MLB College, reassured him, 'Don't worry, Jijaji. I will share my room with him and get him admitted too.' Satisfied, Moolchand returned to his village.

Having failed class twelve in the mathematics stream, Manoj had successfully reappeared for the exam, securing 55 per cent opting for a different set of papers—history, Hindi literature and political science. He had managed to secure the passing mark in the mandatory English paper too. As he was setting out for Gwalior, his mother had somehow arranged Rs 2000 for him. Over the past one year, Manoj's father had been mostly away, returning home only once. The auto was still parked outside the police station, neglected and awaiting the court's verdict.

Manoj succeeded in getting admission into MLB College. The college operated out of an impressive British-era building, near Achleshwar Temple. When Triloki told him that Atal Bihari Vajpayee was among the distinguished alumni of the college, Manoj was mighty impressed. He considered himself fortunate to be a part of an institution with such a legacy. Triloki lived in Lalitpur colony, near Shankar Chowk. The college was not too far away.

The college had a healthy academic ambience. Following a few early days of unfamiliarity, both with the place and its people, the students soon began mingling with each another. Manoj noticed that they were two kinds of students in the college. The first category comprised students from nearby villages. Vikas Bhadauria and Ravikant Dwivedi belonged to this category. The second group comprised Gwalior-based students. Compared to the village boys, they were affluent and rode to college on a scooter or a Hero Puch. Amit Dikshit and Manish belonged to this second group. There was yet another trait specific to this group: all of them had studied mathematics and biology in class twelve. Having failed engineering or medical entrance exams, they were now trying out the arena of arts.

One day, students from both groups somehow gathered at a platform near a tree—attendance in class was thus quite sparse. Although by now they knew one another fairly well, that day they opened up and shared their personal stories. Asked about his past, Manish replied, 'I studied biology in class twelve and managed 70 per cent. But since I couldn't clear the medical entrance, I enrolled for a BA degree. I'll now prepare for the PSC exam.'

Vikas Bhadauria had other plans. 'I want to be a TV reporter, covering all the big breaking news in India and abroad. One day, you will see me on the TV, I can tell you that,' he said, running his fingers through his curly hair.

'I am sure you will; you have my best wishes,' responded Manoj. Bhadauria was elated at the good wishes. 'Thank you, Manoj bhai,' he beamed.

Ravikant Dwivedi was a student of English literature and wanted to be a college teacher. It was now Manoj's turn to speak. Manoj found them all to be very intelligent and smart; most of them had secured a first division in class twelve. Compared to them, he was a simple villager whom no one took seriously. He feared that were he to tell them the truth—that he had barely passed in the arts stream with 55 per cent marks, having once failed in mathematics—he would be chucked out of that group of talented boys. As someone who believed that keeping company with bright students was the key to progress, Manoj was not prepared to reveal his story. 'I too had mathematics,' he said. 'My percentage, however, is a little less: it's sixty-five.'

Manoj could not dare to inflate his marks to 70 per cent. He remained content with sixty-five and got himself drafted into the group. Since no one was going to ask for his marksheet, there was no fear of getting exposed.

When Amit Dikshit's turn came, he created a sensation of sorts. 'Getting into the state PSC is beneath my standards. I will become an Indian Police Service officer; only the police uniform suits my personality. I want an exciting life, full of thrills,' he declared.

Everyone seemed in awe of Amit as they pictured him looking dapper as an IPS officer in a police uniform. Manoj was impressed too. Just then, a man with a booming voice interrupted the meeting. 'Why are you all gossiping during lecture hours?' It was Principal Govind Sharma. Everyone froze in fear, too scared to make another sound. Finally, Bhadauria showed a little courage and said, 'Sir, our political science professor is on leave today; his period was free.'

The principal knew that a bunch of students chattering noisily on the campus would not only disrupt ongoing classes, but would also cause the chatterers to fall into the bad habit of wasting time in idle talk. 'Go to your class,' he said in a firm tone, 'I will join you in a moment.'

As they returned to class, Manoj made sure to sit next to Amit—the smartest and the most ambitious of the lot. He was keen to befriend him. But Amit had no intention of becoming chummy with an emaciated villager and quit his seat to join Manish, a city boy like himself. Manoj could only shrivel at the humiliation.

Principal Sir was a man on a mission. He wasted no time in worthless discussion and started with his lecture straight away. 'Has anyone here read about Marxism?'

Nobody had an answer. Most of them had completed their higher secondary education in science and mathematics, Marxism was Greek to them. Even Amit Dikshit—the boy who had boasted of getting into the IPS a short while ago—had no answer. A humbling silence echoed through the class. But Manoj had read about Karl Marx in his political science textbook. If he answered, he knew it would prove his worth to both the principal and the class. He mustered a little courage and raised his hand.

'Well, I am relieved to see that in a class this big at least one student has heard of Marx. What is your name?' asked the principal.

'Manoj Kumar Sharma.' It was spoken loudly enough for everyone to hear.

'Excellent, Manoj. Tell us what you know.'

'Sir, there are two kinds of people in the world—the rich and the poor. Since the rich are greedy and exploit the poor, the latter must snatch their rights back from the former. This is what Marx has taught us.' Whatever he could recall, however fragmented, he said it all.

'In this analysis, the rich are the capitalists and the poor are called the proletariat. Very good, Manoj. You may sit,' said the principal. Thereafter, he spoke on Marxism for nearly half an hour. Manoj sat mesmerized throughout the lecture, listening to the principal with rapt attention. Once the class got over, Ravikant Dwivedi and Bhadauria congratulated him.

'It seems to me that we villagers—even though we come from different villages—are the proletariat,' said Bhadauria, 'while these city-born, motorcycle-riding smarties are the capitalists. Today, you have rescued our collective pride.' Manoj's face lit up with happiness at the compliment.

10

Manoj spent his first few months looking for a foothold in Gwalior. After paying the college fee and purchasing textbooks, he was left with little extra money. It was already his third month living with Triloki. At the time that Manoj had moved in, Triloki was already sharing his room with Keshav. Although Triloki had no issues with three people living in a room meant for two, Keshav was not so cool about it. However, since Manoj was Triloki's relative, he could not ask him to move out. Keshav was pursuing a Bachelor of Science degree and was always seen with a book in his hands. He looked down on Manoj, a student of the arts. But one day, after struggling with the thought for a long time, he finally spoke his mind. 'Manoj, you should look for another room; with three people staying together, my studies are getting hampered.'

Manoj assured him that he would soon rent a room. However, when Triloki learnt of it, he took Keshav to task and spoke firmly. 'I am sure three people can easily fit into this room. Also, since Manoj is new to Gwalior, he will spend his first year with me: let this be clear to you.' Although Keshav could not register his protest, from that day onwards, he developed an intense dislike for Manoj.

One morning, Triloki set out for his village on some errand. Manoj too left for college, leaving Keshav alone in the room. Since one of the periods was free, Manoj and Ravikant decided to sit in the college grounds and discuss the prospect of doing a BA with English literature.

Ravikant was quick to list the advantages of English. 'These days, nothing is possible without English. Good English is a must for a good life.'

The mere mention of English was enough to scare the wits out of Manoj. 'It isn't so important for the PSC,' he argued.

'But it's an essential life skill. Besides, whoever has guaranteed you success in the PSC exam? If you don't make it through, playing the jhunjhuna of Hindi will not help you keep your body and soul together. Good English opens up numerous opportunities. You can give tuitions for a start. English teachers are always in great demand at all schools and colleges,' said Ravikant, firm in his belief.

Faced with the stark reality, Manoj panicked. What if he wasn't selected for the PSC? He hadn't weighed the possibility.

'Manoj bhai, you've already committed the mistake of pursuing a worthless subject like the arts. In this day and age, it won't earn you a living. English is your last hope. If you learn it well, you can somehow secure your future,' claimed Ravikant. Given how the market determines our future, Ravikant's assessment was spot on. Convinced by the rationale, Manoj decided to opt for English literature besides Hindi and history. The discussions went on till four in the evening that day.

When Manoj reached his room, he saw a lock dangling from the door. Since he didn't have any other place to go to, he decided to stay put and wait for his roommate. However, when Keshav did not show up even after two hours, he grew worried. Finally, he went to a friend of Keshav's, who lived nearby, and was shocked to learn that his roommate had gone to his village.

11

Triloki's room was locked, its keys were with Keshav. Where was Manoj supposed to spend the night? In that big a city, with those many houses, Manoj kept looking for shelter. But there was no refuge in sight. He was hungry too. With the Rs 20 left in his pocket, he ate a plate of chhole-bhature.

It was going to be a long and tough night. Suddenly, he was reminded of Bhadauria, who lived not too far away at Rajput Boarding. But misfortune never comes alone, as they say: Bhadauria too had gone to his village. In all of Gwalior, there wasn't a single relative or friend who would shelter him for the night. Tired of the ordeal, he sat on the steps of Achleshwar Temple near the college. That day, he came to realize what a luxury it was to have a room of one's own. He spent the night observing the beggars on the footpath across the road— emaciated women and old, infirm men, clutching their rags, getting ready to sleep.

That sight made him forget all about his own worries. This was his first night being homeless, but for those poor beggars on the road, it was a way of life. What did the world mean to them, he wondered. What made them happy? What did they want from life? There were a few infants too, suckling at their mother's breast. Were they destined to live on the footpath even when they grew up? Manoj spent the night grappling with these difficult questions.

Although the beggars slept off after a while, he did not sleep at all. He felt as if he had shared both their journey and pain. Would he ever have the capability to help these homeless?

When morning dawned, he washed his face at the municipal tap, drank a little water and proceeded to the park near Katora Lake. Since he had not slept at all, he dozed off as soon as he settled on a bench. He woke up two hours later, feeling somewhat rejuvenated. Throughout the day, he kept returning to his room, only to find the door locked. There was no money left on him. He spent most of his time in the college and returned to the park at night on an empty stomach.

Suddenly, while sitting on a bench, a thought occurred to him—such difficulties were inevitable and they would challenge him to rise to the occasion. However difficult the times were, his patience must never wear thin. Regardless of everything, he must keep studying hard. Out of the blue, he felt a surge of courage in his heart. The next morning, he arose and left for his classes, quick on his feet. Thereafter, he attended three lectures, one after the other. He decided that he would never weep or beg for rescue, never ask friends for help. Manoj was convinced that success would come to him only if he dared to walk down the difficult path and not the easy one. He was beginning to experience an odd pleasure in facing adversities.

It was night again. For the past two days, not a morsel had entered his belly. Extreme hunger had wearied his body. He feared that if he starved any longer, he would surely faint. After a brief walk, he reached Savitri Bhojnalaya in Lalitpur colony. Its thirty-year-old owner was sitting at the counter. Manoj approached him and said bluntly, 'I do not have money. Can I work for a meal?'

Manoj's question oozed confidence; it wasn't a meek request. The owner looked him up and down—his clothes were dirty and loosely fitted, his frail and lean face was bearded, and his eyes sunken. He turned Manoj's request over in his mind and replied, 'I already have people who work for me.'

Although disappointed, Manoj held on to a slender hope and pressed forth with his proposal. 'I need to eat. And because I do not have money, I am willing to work as a labourer.'

The bhojnalaya served hundreds of students every day. Many, who did not have money, ate on credit. On several occasions, the bill was never paid. There were also those who simply made a sorry face and ate for free. The eatery's owner knew the boys inside out. However, he had never met someone like Manoj, or heard such an offer. He summoned a waiter and ordered, 'A thali for this bhaisahib here.'

Soon a full platter with lentil soup, cauliflower curry, five chapattis and rice arrived. Manoj blanked out briefly at the spectacle. For a starving boy, it was an astonishing ordinary meal, earned under circumstances equally fascinating. Perhaps for the first time in his life, Manoj realized how difficult it was to keep oneself nourished. His eyes brimmed over with tears. He was also quite moved by the owner's kindness. Having finished his dinner, he approached the owner and said, 'Thank you. Now please assign me work. I can do everything.'

'You have had your food; that's enough. You don't need to work to repay.'

As Manoj was talking to the owner, Ravikant arrived at the eatery. When he heard Manoj's story, he took out Rs 30 from his wallet and tried to pay the bill. However, Manoj was firm on working. Everyone present at the restaurant marvelled at the spectacle—a lean, bearded boy was firm on working for his meal, the owner would not let him work, and another boy stood waiting with money in his hands, keen to pay for his friend's dinner. Ravikant had never imagined that a boy so calm and unassuming at the college could also be so stubborn.

It seemed as if Manoj was in a state of inebriation, his mind fixated on a single thought. He had no idea how or why he came to be seized by that stubbornness. 'If you do not let me work, I'll keep standing here. If you shut the gates, I will stand outside and wait. I'll keep on waiting till you permit me to work for you.'

Having spent three days on the streets, Manoj did not mind waiting. Toughened by his ordeal, he could stand firm till the owner relented. The owner didn't know quite what to do. Ravikant was equally baffled as he stood waiting with money in his hand. A few at the eatery laughed at the drama. Others felt that Manoj was either too much of an idealist or a complete idiot. Exhausted, the owner summoned a servant and said, 'Take this bhaisahib with you. He'll do the dishes.'

The servants were also astounded. In the past, many had eaten for free. Others ate on credit and disappeared. But the owner had never forced a customer to clean dirty plates before. Although the eatery was his sole source of livelihood, he never hounded a student for money. Yet, the venture earned him enough profit. Today, once again, the owner had to submit to a young man's doggedness, albeit under different circumstances.

When he repeated his command, the servant escorted Manoj towards the kitchen. Manoj worked for nearly thirty minutes. Outside, Ravikant waited patiently for his friend. Finally, Manoj returned to the counter and thanked the owner profusely: 'I am truly grateful for the meal.'

His eyes glowed with pride as he uttered those words. The owner got up from his chair and moved to the front. He saw Manoj off, shaking his hand near the exit. Perhaps he wanted to say something too, but could not. Ravikant took Manoj back with him, to his room.

12

He gently rebuked Manoj, 'You have been homeless for three days. You should have told me about your problem.'

Manoj was overwhelmed with emotion. 'You see, these experiences make me strong. What is there to grumble about? Besides, there are countless who sleep under the open sky. Many others sleep on an empty stomach. Over the three days, I have felt closer to the poor and the destitute—the proletariat, as Marx calls them. We should be faithful to this class. You know something, the experience of being among the most oppressed and powerless is going to be my strength.'

Manoj analysed his own experience in the light of his principal's lecture on Marxism. For the next two days, he stayed with Ravikant. Tiwari Sir, one of Ravikant's teachers, lived near the market. He had rented a hall from which he ran classes for spoken English, and grammar. Ravikant had a plan. 'Forget about others. Tiwari Sir is looking for a room partner. You can split the rent; it's five hundred. He will also teach you English.' Manoj liked the proposal. He collected his suitcase and mattress from Triloki's room, and shifted to Tiwari Sir's room.

Tiwari Sir was a short thirty-year-old man, who wore thick, black-framed glasses and—having spent long hours sitting in the coaching class—had grown a belly. When Manoj reached his room, Tiwari Sir was resting on the bed, worn out after a long day at work. Manoj wasted no time and touched his feet. After all, Tiwari Sir was to be his English teacher too. Manoj knew that his English was destined to get better.

Manoj laid out his mattress on the floor. It was like a portrait from the scriptures: Guru Vyas on his bed, the disciple at his feet. Manoj had found a permanent room and an English teacher, while Tiwari Sir had bargained on an obedient helping hand. In no time, Manoj settled into a new routine. Each morning, at seven, he served a glass of warm milk to his guruji. Thereafter, he cooked food—two meals every day.

Each evening, as guruji got back from his coaching centre, he would simply stretch out on the bed. One evening, Manoj came up with a request: 'Guruji, please help me with *Macbeth*; I can't make head or tail of the play.'

'I surely will. But today I'm exhausted; my feet ache so badly. Listen, why don't you give me a foot massage?' he asked, feigning fatigue.

Manoj had no reservations about being of service to his guru. The door to knowledge can only be reached through the corridors of selfless service—this he knew. In fact, he wanted to exceed his guruji's expectations. He fetched a bucket of warm water for Tiwari Sir to dip his feet in, and started massaging them enthusiastically. The gesture moved his guru into making a generous offer. 'Before you graduate to literature, it is important to master grammar and English speech. Tomorrow onwards, come for the 7 p.m. class. It's a new batch with students of your age,' he said, while relishing the treatment fit for the kings.

It was indeed a useful proposal. Since Manoj did not have to pay a fee, guruji decided to stop washing his clothes. Each morning before bathing, Manoj washed guruji's outer wear and undergarments, and each evening, he attended the English classes. But he soon discovered that the classes were somewhat underwhelming.

In a sixty-minute class, only fifteen minutes were spent on real teaching. It was more of a fashionable gathering in the name of English. Guruji would start off with the present tense, but even after three months of regular lectures, the class had only reached as far as future tense, via a short detour through past tense. As a rule, guruji brought an English magazine or a newspaper to the class. The students would read aloud from it and guruji would interpret their reading. Guruji knew that learning English was an endless process; to learn a foreign language, one needed to go slow. That is why neither guruji nor his students were in any hurry whatsoever.

In a class of ten, there were four girls and six boys. Manoj had already spent a month with them, yet his struggle with the present tense raged on. He could not distinguish between 'he goes' and 'he is going'. There were boys who had spent almost a year with guruji. However, in terms of achievement, they only had lady-loves to show for the time spent there. The girls in the class were no better. Thus, guruji's institute had blossomed into a centre for love. There were no girls at MLB College or boys at KRG College; so all the love-starved souls convened at the centre.

By setting up his coaching centre, guruji had done an incalculable favour to the 'department of amorous affairs' in Gwalior. Since guruji had made all the investment in the coaching centre, he felt he had the first right to fall in love, ahead of all his students. Each year, he had an average of two or three affairs.

One day, a girl walked up to him and announced, 'Sir today is Mona's birthday.' Mona was pursuing a BSc from KRG College. The previous batch had graduated without making any real progress with English. Guruji's old flames from earlier batches were already living with their in-laws by now. He, therefore, felt the urgent need to fall in love with Mona.

The lady, however, was indifferent to him. But guruji was a seasoned lover; he knew that a birthday was a great occasion to launch a new affair. Desperate for love, he interrupted the class, which was anyway moving at a snail's pace, and said, 'It's Mona's birthday; yet I see no excitement in class.'

Before long, a boy was commissioned to get kachoris and jalebis for the entire class from SS Kachori Centre. Of late, Mona had started casting lovelorn glances at Manoj. She couldn't help admiring his innocence. She remained on the lookout for the slightest of opportunities to interact with him, often using notebooks, magazines or even a pen as a pretext. Now she said, 'This is for you,' bringing the snacks to him.

'Happy birthday,' responded Manoj.

'Thanks,' said Mona, the hint of a smile playing on her lips. For Mona, Manoj's warm wishes had brightened her day. It seemed as if Manoj was reaping profits on an investment made by guruji. As for guruji, it wasn't his first brush with losses.

Although the route Manoj took to go back to his room ran opposite to Mona's, but one day after class they dared to walk together. Although Manoj was dying to talk to Mona, he struggled to come up with a conversation-worthy subject. Finally, he broke the ice with a rather plain question: 'What do you plan to do after BSc? Will you be preparing for the PSC exam?'

'No, I want to get married,' she said.

Manoj had expected a different answer. After walking quietly for a while, they reached the lane that led to Mona's house. As Mona left, Manoj stood frozen watching her till she disappeared.

A few days later, a boy told everyone in the class that it was Manoj's birthday and the birthday boy would throw a party. Treating the entire class to samosas and jalebis on one's birthday was an unscripted rule. But Manoj had run out of money and said simply, 'I can't throw a party tomorrow; I have no money.'

Since there were no samosas in the offing, nobody wished him
on his birthday. However, Mona had secretly made arrangements
for the day, taking Manoj and the others by surprise. Naturally,
guruji took offence at this. He burned with envy and was livid
with Manoj. At the end of the class, Mona gave a greeting
card to Manoj. There was a red heart imprinted on it, across
which Mona had scribbled a birthday wish in her beautiful
handwriting—'Happy Birthday, Man'. Mona had conferred a
secret new name on Manoj—one to which only she was privy.
Perhaps, in her heart of hearts, she often hummed the name.

That night, when Tiwari Sir returned to the room, Manoj
was sitting on a chair. For months now, he had been diligent
in serving all of his guruji's wishes, but all of it was soon to be
of no avail. Seething with envy, Tiwari Sir started abusing his
roommate. And when the foul-mouthed ranting did not cool
him down, he vented his ire on Manoj's belongings, breaking
both his heater and earthen pitcher. Mona's card was lying on a
table. He grabbed it violently, tore it to pieces and asked Manoj
to vacate the room at the earliest.

Manoj broke down at this unexpectedly hostile treatment,
collected his possessions and stepped out of the room. As soon
as he was out, Tiwari Sir slammed the door shut.

Scarred by the experience, Manoj decided to return to
his village, hoping to spend a few days with his family. His
father had not come home in months. However, he had done
well to send a little money, easing the family's financial stress.
Stranded at the police station, the tempo was on the verge of
becoming a wreck; the court had no time to take a call on its fate.
Meanwhile, Pandit Kalicharan had started hounding the family
for loan repayment.

13

The day he was to return to Gwalior from his village, his mother gave him a thousand rupees. His first-year examinations had drawn near. Back from village, he rented a shanty in Tope Wale Muhallah, near the Jeevajigunj drain. Ever since he had moved out of Tiwari Sir's room, he hadn't met Mona. The two never met again—neither in a city as big as Gwalior, nor in a world so small.

In no time, Manoj became chummy with all and sundry in his new locality. To earn praise from his neighbours, he would light a lamp and study on his terrace till late at night. There were days when the grind went on till four or five in the morning. Soon, the neighbourhood women started telling their good-for-nothing children to take inspiration from him. If Manoj were to earn respect and acceptance in Gwalior, education was his only recourse.

Soon the exams were over and the results were declared. Manoj had scored a lowly 55 per cent. His performance in English literature—which he had barely passed—had brought his aggregate down. He left for his village to spend the summer break at home and returned after a month for the second year of his BA.

It was a December afternoon when Ravikant came up with a proposition. 'Manoj, would you like to go for a three-day youth motivation camp at the Vivekananda Kendra?'

Before Manoj could respond, Ravikant lavished praise on
the organization and said, 'The Kendra encourages youth to be
patriotic and work for social welfare. I know these ideas interest
you; you must come.'

Manoj was indeed impressed with the idea. This ashram-like
centre was located atop a hillock near Gwalior. He paid the
Rs 100 registration fee and on the designated day, reached the
centre along with Ravikant. The next morning at around five, the
activities commenced.

A day in camp began with a Sanskrit prayer for universal
happiness—'*Sarve Bhavantu Sukhinah*'. This was followed by
yoga. Thereafter, scholars from Gwalior lectured attendees on
inspirational lives of legends from India. The evening sessions
were reserved for group discussions. The campers debated on
topics such as 'terrorism', 'the road ahead for the country's youth'
and 'women empowerment'. Manoj enthusiastically participated
in all activities.

He had finally found a community that seemed well-read
and talented. Manoj was excited. Not only did he want to
learn a great deal in their company, he also hoped to make an
impression on them with his abilities. In fact, he wanted to earn
the certificate for the best participant. To this end, he often took
the lead in group discussions as well as post-lecture question-
and-answer sessions. When it came to voluntary labour, he did
not lag behind either. His indomitable quest for plaudits was his
greatest strength.

On the second day of the camp, he made the following entry
in his diary:

Never before in my life have I experienced such joy. There
is something about these people here who call themselves
social workers. They inspire me to contribute my bit

to nation-building. I'm quite impressed with Rajneesh Tyagi—undoubtedly a great guy. He is a principal at a certain school in Gwalior. The way he lectured on the life of Swami Vivekananda was totally mesmerizing; I've never heard anything quite like that. I felt drenched in a profound sense of purity. Vivekananda says that there is no greater a sin than calling oneself weak. Coming here, I have come to realize that I can achieve anything I want in life; I am filled with boundless strength. There is no greater a faith than one's nation and there could be no greater a purpose than serving it. I have pledged that serving our nation shall be lifelong mission.

Manoj was quite enthralled by the Kendra, its ideology, as well as its staff. Tyagiji came up with a scheme that required the volunteers to go around the city every Sunday, collecting winter clothes and then distributing them amongst the poor. Till now, Manoj had only heard lectures on patriotism; this was his first time participating in a truly patriotic act.

Finally, the camp came to an end. Manoj was adjudged the best participant. The recognition brought him the opportunity to share his thoughts from the stage. Speaking from the podium, Manoj took a solemn pledge that he would lead an honest life and serve his nation. His emotional vow was met with resounding applause. The ovation, as always, boosted his confidence.

He spent the next Sunday collecting old clothes to distribute to the needy. At the end of the day, he put down his thoughts in his diary.

I managed to collect enough clothes. Some of the donors treated me with respect, while a few tried to put me down. I was pained to see those scenes of utter poverty; the desperation with which people flocked to me, impatient for discarded clothes. Oh God! How will they survive? Tyagiji was right—moving door to door for donation will not only puncture our bloated ego but will also make us realize how very important the society is, and how very insignificant individuals are.

He was clear in his head that he had to contribute his bit for the well-being of society. The certificate he had earned at the Vivekananda Kendra was placed next to God's idol.

14

Manoj set aside his textbooks and started devouring *Vivekananda Sahitya*. The second-year examination was around the corner, but serving his country was all he could think of. Were he to pursue this new-found mission, he had to associate himself with the Vivekananda Kendra; of that, he was certain. Gradually, Manoj began drifting away from his long-standing dream of getting into the PSC. Instead, he felt a strong urge to dedicate his life to the Kendra. Possessed by these thoughts, he appeared for his college exams and got a second division. Once again, he barely passed the English literature paper.

In the summer break, he again left for his village. Once home, he started preparing for his final-year examinations. In September, he went for another programme at the Vivekananda Kendra: a rigorous fifteen-day camp. He returned all energized and sat down to record his experiences in his diary.

I tried reading Vivekananda literature. So far, I have managed only six or seven books. However, I feel completely drained; I do not have the courage to read any further. My mind is on fire, my body burns with passion. Whether awake or asleep, I am crazed by a desire to work for the Kendra—a desire so strong, growing with such strength, that the day when I surrender my very existence to the nation doesn't seem too far away.

For the next ten–fifteen days, smitten by his new mission, he felt a great churning in his heart. But before long, he ran out of money and returned to his village. Perplexed by his father's long absence, his mother had left for Dindori, taking Rajni with her. Since the house was empty, Manoj went to Rakesh's home. He wanted to share everything with his friend—his dilemma as well as his new mission. But the moment he told Rakesh that he wanted to serve the Kendra instead of focusing on the PSC, Rakesh turned solemn and asked, 'So, you won't prepare for PSC any more?'

'Serving the country is now my only objective. I want to dedicate my life to the downtrodden of this country,' answered Manoj.

'Does that mean you'll leave your home? And your family too?'

'For me, the entire country is one big family,' replied Manoj, completely under the spell of the Vivekananda Kendra.

Although it was getting difficult to talk Manoj out of his resolution, Rakesh kept trying. 'Don't you know your father well enough? If you too abandon the family, who will arrange for Rajni's marriage? Who'll provide for the family?'

'You see, every girl in this country is my sister, and every woman my mother.' Manoj was full of passion. The spirit of service had taken hold of his soul. Rakesh, on the other hand, was busy hammering common sense into his head.

'What about the SDMs and the thanedars? Don't they serve the nation too? Don't you remember how SDM Dushyant disciplined the thanedar and released Mukesh? Isn't that social service too? If the thanedar were honest, would he have confiscated your tempo? Certainly not! We desperately need good and honest people at police stations and courts. And here you are, thinking of quitting your PSC dream. Have you lost the courage to work hard? Don't make excuses.'

The truth that Rakesh spoke was getting increasingly bitter for Manoj to digest. He was challenging Manoj's abilities. As soon as Rakesh sensed that his friend was on the back foot, he upped the ante and said, 'If you really wish to serve the nation, you must clear the PSC. The ashrams are full of idlers who have run away from their responsibilities.'

Manoj had no clue how Rakesh was so well-armed with logic to dismantle his scheme; he only felt a great turbulence grow in his head. The words of caution that Rakesh uttered were beginning to tell on him, as Manoj could see the truth they laid bare.

'You are right. Running away from the PSC would be an act of cowardice. People would say that I quit since I never had the pluck to compete in it. I must first put my abilities to test. It is resolved; I'll serve the country by becoming a PSC officer.'

Manoj had decided to return to the road he had gone astray from, his inner conflict stood resolved. Hereafter, clearing the PSC exam was to be his main goal.

Since his parents had not yet returned from Dindori, he decided to pay them a visit himself. Once there, he learnt that his father had been suspended and was getting only half his salary. The money was barely enough to feed the family. When asked about the whole affair, his father launched a fierce harangue and said, 'I will destroy the deputy director. I won't admit defeat. I am an honest man. They are all corrupt; I'll take them to task. I have written to the prime minister too. Only the high court will get me justice.'

But Manoj's mother wasn't impressed with the outburst. 'He doesn't know how to keep his job. The entire world works;

performing one's duties is not a miracle. All that he has ever known is how to pick a fight. He misbehaves with his officers and in the middle of a packed meeting, takes his slippers off to thrash the deputy director. If he doesn't get suspended, who will?'

Manoj's father didn't like the revelation. 'You know nothing. They are looting the money meant for poor farmers. Corrupt people like them deserve a sound thrashing.'

But today, his mother had no plan to lose the duel. 'They remain unaffected while we are completely gutted. Our son doesn't have money for his college fees. Our girl ... Well, have you ever spared a thought for our girl's marriage? And then there is the forty-thousand rupee debt that weighs us down.'

'Had I not warned you about the tempo?' It was his father's turn to prove his point. 'We were never cut out for that enterprise. But look at you: you are so fond of interfering in my fight for justice.'

The debate remained inconclusive. However, Manoj was impressed with his father's quest for justice.

On his way back, sitting in the general compartment of the train, he kept thinking about his father. 'You're on the correct path, Papa. You are fighting a battle for truth. To pull you down is like trying to seal the mouth of a fire-spewing volcano.' In the light of whatever he had learnt about honesty and patriotism at the Vivekananda Kendra, his father's actions appeared completely justified.

15

Manoj was back in Gwalior for his final-year examinations. So far, he had absolutely no clue what or how to read for the PSC exam. He was totally ignorant about the strategy one needed to clear the preliminary exam—the prelims; let alone the mains, or the final interview. There was no senior around him either who had cleared the lot; he was yet to find students who were serious about the PSC.

Then one day, Manish told him of a senior who had cleared the prelims and was now preparing hard for the mains. Manoj couldn't let this opportunity pass. Deep Soni, the senior, lived in a building near Harkishan Puram. The two-storeyed structure, painted bright yellow, was famous as Peelikothi throughout Gwalior. There were about a dozen rooms in the building, each occupied by a PSC aspirant. Several of these aspirants had their own home in Gwalior, but had left to study here in peace. Peelikothi provided them with the best atmosphere, and each year, at least four or five of the students staying there cleared their mains. The residents of this hallowed building were known to study in groups and to exchange notes—the key to their success in the PSC.

The two friends reached Deep's room. It was ten in the morning and the door was closed. As Manish raised his hand to knock, he noticed a slip pasted on the door. It was Deep's time-table, which read as follows:

From 10 a.m. to 5 p.m.: study

From 8 p.m. to 4 a.m.: study
From 4 a.m. to 10 a.m.: sleep

Manish read it aloud. As per the schedule, it was time for Deep to get up. Within minutes, sharp at ten, the door opened and the two were summoned inside. There was no place to sit; books lay scattered all over the bed: some open, others closed. The walls were covered with different maps: of Madhya Pradesh, India and the world. At places, a few notes were stuck too, with details of fundamental rights, royal dynasties, deficiency-borne diseases, etc., scribbled on them. Important passages from books were highlighted in many colours—yellow, orange and blue—making the pages glow like a rainbow. Pushing away the scattered stationery, the two friends managed to sit on the edge of the bed.

Manoj was stunned by the condition of the room, which mirrored Deep's hard labour; he had never seen anyone study with such fervour. Compared to Deep's monumental efforts, signs of which were writ large all over the room, Manoj's own labour seemed like a baby step.

'What are your subjects in PSC?' asked Manoj, initiating the discussion.

'Chemistry and history,' answered Deep.

Manoj too had opted for history. When asked about the history books one must read to clear the prelims, Deep dictated a long list of about ten books. And when asked about the study plan, he painted a scary picture of a life of severe discipline and said, 'If you want to get selected, you must put in eighteen hours of study every day. You have to forget all about rest and eating. Friends, fun, films, drama, family functions and relatives: you need to stay away from all of these. Look at me. Although my home is quite close to this place, I don't stay there.'

But Manoj craved to know more; he wanted to know the secret to preparing well. 'And what should be one's approach to studies?'

'Just keep studying—without fatigue, without a break, non-stop—and with great patience, in spite of failures. I have read these no less than twenty times,' said Deep, pointing to his books.

Manoj was somewhat worried. 'How many years of labour does it take to become a deputy collector?' he asked. Deep stared at his face and then laughed. 'If you work hard enough, maybe within a year.'

But the doubts that simmered in Manoj's head weren't cleared as yet. 'Did you have mathematics in class twelve? What was your percentage?' he asked, reflecting on his own failure.

'I have been first-divisioner all my life. In fact, I have a scholarship to pursue a PhD in chemistry.'

Manoj was now a little worried, as he compared Deep's abilities to his own, disappointment showed on his face. He was just a minnow. At 10.30 a.m. sharp, Deep picked up his history book and started reading, leaving the two gaping at his discipline. They stood up, said namaste and left. Absorbed in his reading, Deep merely nodded.

Manoj was completely overwhelmed by Deep's illustrious record. However, he tried to boost his own morale by saying, 'The amount of effort that Deep bhaisahib puts in is so deadly; like a ghost he is indifferent to the world. With his kind of seriousness, one will surely get selected within a year. I too shall toil like him.' Through that discourse on hard work, Manoj wanted to forget all about his own poor academic record.

'I too have decided to move to Peelikothi,' replied Manish.

'I will also move here after my BA,' said Manoj, 'and will start preparing seriously.' Both were in awe of the ambience at Peelikothi.

Manoj walked back to his place, lost in thought. On the one hand, he imagined his future preparing for the PSC in Peelikothi, on the other hand, the haunting realization of being a twelfth-fail made him feel small. 'Deep Sir has always been brilliant. Can I ever match him? Will my weak foundation create hurdles for me? Is hard work enough for success? Were I really intelligent, would I have still failed class twelve?' Grappling with these questions, Manoj reached his room.

16

Manoj passed the BA exam scoring 55 per cent. Once again, he had managed only passing marks in English. On the day his result was declared, he made another entry into his diary. 'Now I have to jump into the arena of the PSC exam. I am determined to stay at Peelikothi and work hard.'

Although he was hardly prepared for the PSC exam, yet, with a view to gain experience if nothing more, he thought of appearing for it immediately after his BA result. Madhav College near Nai Sadak was the venue for the prelims. There was a two-hour break after the first paper, which was history. The paper on general studies was scheduled for after the recess. Manoj was sitting on a platform under a tree, poring over a book. Just then, a boy approached him, shook his hand and introduced himself saying, 'Hello, I am Vikramaditya Pandey. It will be easier if you call me just Pandey.' Manoj too introduced himself with a smile.

'How was the paper?' Pandey asked, but did not wait for a reply and went on speaking. 'Well, when a student steps out of the exam hall, ninety of the hundred questions are usually correct. However, once the answers are checked, the number of correct responses depletes fast.'

Pandey drew his attention to a boy reading through a fellow aspirant's responses. He was ruthless in striking out questions previously marked as correct and spoke quite condescendingly. 'I can't believe you botched up a question this easy, I could have answered it even in my sleep. The correct option is "A", not "C".

Brother, your chances of clearing the prelims seems terribly slim. But you are always welcome to my room if you ever need any guidance.'

Pandey shouted across to the boy. 'Gupta, come here for a moment. How was your paper?'

Since Gupta was from Bundelkhand, Pandey spoke to him in the Bundelkhandi dialect. Last year, Gupta had cleared the prelims. Naturally, he oozed confidence. 'It was great; brilliant. Consider it done.'

Gupta too shook hands with Manoj and introduced himself, 'I am Mukul Gupta. I cleared the prelims last year. Had I not missed the mains by a few marks, by now I would have been a deputy collector somewhere.'

Pandey was irritated by Gupta's big-headedness. Cutting him short, he said, 'That is an old story, Gupta. Tell me about today's paper.'

'Ninety answers are correct, ten are doubtful,' replied Gupta, considerably excited.

Pandey took Gupta's paper and started reviewing his answers. 'Chandragupta did not establish Gupta dynasty; it was established by Shrigupta. This is wrong. And look here, another mistake; it was Balban not Allaudin Khilji, who introduced the policy of "blood and iron".'

Quite effortlessly, Pandey had spotted fifteen mistakes in Gupta's paper. But Gupta was not ready to concede. He snatched the paper back and said, 'I will check later, once I reach my room. Why should I trust you? Although I know my answers are right, however, for now, I am ready to mark them as doubtful.' Once Gupta left, Pandey summarized his character by saying, 'An empty vessel makes more noise.'

Over time, Manoj started enjoying his conversations with Pandey. He also shared his address thinking Pandey was a good student and would help him in studies. Pandey's own room wasn't too far off from Manoj's. He started visiting Manoj every two or three days. Soon, the two became good friends.

Manoj's father was still under suspension. But misfortune never comes alone, and soon after his suspension he was transferred to Jhabua. However, when he refused to leave Dindori—because he considered the official diktat a grievous insult—his already-halved salary was also discontinued. The family was in dire straits, and Manoj's monthly allowance of Rs 1,000 had to be stopped. It was a terrible beginning to a time he had hoped to utilize for the PSC exam.

He had dreamt of shifting to Peelikothi, but now living in Gwalior itself seemed impossible. One needed at least Rs 1,000 a month to live at Peelikothi, but he could no longer count on his family. However, instead of cursing fate, Manoj was determined to weather the storm by giving tuitions and earning enough to rent a room at Peelikothi.

Manoj shared his hardships with Pandey. He told him about his father's suspension and the family's financial struggle, projecting his father as a hero. He had hoped that Pandey would extol his father's greatness and bestow respect on him for being the son of such a great man, but his friend's reaction surprised him.

'Your father is destroying himself by giving in to his bloated ego,' Pandey replied. 'He is concerned about everything, except his wife and children. To me, he seems like a deluded man who considers himself great and dismisses others as pathetic. If you were to ask me, abandon all your hopes of getting help from him.'

Manoj did not quite approve of Pandey's assessment. 'You have no idea how perilous the righteous path is, Pandey,' he said. 'My father's soul is pure like twenty-four carat gold; he is an honest man.' Pandey merely curled his lip in a sneer, but decided against answering back.

The next day, Manoj went around knocking at every door in Ratan colony, asking every family if they required tuitions. A few women turned him away saying they had no kids. One woman told him that her son was in class ten, and needed a tutor for mathematics and physics—subjects Manoj was particularly bad at. Another wanted a tutor for a boy studying in class seven at an English-medium school. But how could Manoj manage that!

Even after several days of tirelessly foraying around, Manoj could not secure a single tuition. This triggered a crisis of confidence. Distraught, he began doubting his own abilities and in a fit of rage, took out his diary and wrote:

> I always considered myself talented, but today I have come to realize how very useless I am. I have no right to dream big. I was mistaken in imagining myself as talented as Deep Sir. If I can't manage one hundred-rupee worth tuition, can I ever qualify for PSC?

It was evening. Manoj sat on the terrace, staring listlessly at the sky, his body and spirit drained of all energy. He had a fever. Just then, Pandey arrived. Manoj greeted him with a faded smile. For a while, both sat quietly. Pandey picked up Manoj's diary and read its very last page. After a while, he said, 'You don't look too well. You should cook khichadi today.' That was all the help he offered.

Manoj had been secretly hoping for at least some empathy from his friend. However, when he left without uttering a word of consolation, Manoj concluded that the city boys were thoroughly insensitive and least bothered about the sufferings of others. Manoj had lost contact with his college friends too. He felt lonesome in Gwalior.

By morning, his fever got worse, but he had no money to consult a doctor. The following afternoon, when his fever refused to abate, he somehow reached Jain Clinic. As he approached the doctor's table, he decided to be candid about his position. 'Sir, I do not have money for your fee.'

He had hoped that impressed by his honesty and moved by his tragedy, the doctor would treat him for free. But he wasn't as kind and straightforward as the young owner of Savitri Bhojnalaya. The doctor chased Manoj out of his clinic. Badly shaken by the experience, Manoj wondered how a man in such a noble profession could be so heartless.

Left with no choice but to return to his village, he reached Ghosipur narrow-gauge railway station and boarded a train. He could not afford a ticket. Drowsy with fever, he had no idea how he reached his village after the three-hour train journey.

17

Within a few days, Manoj had recovered. One day, his mother told him to return. 'You should go back to Gwalior and focus on your studies. As you know, we have no money. Besides, we have to pay back Pandit Kalicharan too. If your father gets reinstated, perhaps things will get easier for us. I have five-hundred rupees with me. You keep it.' Mother was strong-willed, but helpless. Her courage moved Manoj to tears.

Before leaving for Gwalior, Manoj told Rakesh all about his hardships. His friend too encouraged him to persevere. 'Whatever happens, do not abandon your studies,' he told Manoj. 'Life won't remain so bleak forever. I know these hardships will also give you strength.' Manoj felt a wave of love for Rakesh; he was so different from the friends he had in the city. Unlike Pandey, who was completely indifferent to his woes, Rakesh was greatly concerned. With that thought, he hugged Rakesh affectionately.

He returned to Gwalior, fully resolved that no matter what he would find a job, rent a room at Peelikothi, study hard and get selected within a year. This time, he approached a few private schools, but to no avail. It was the second day following his return, and Manoj already felt weighed down by his financial woes. How could he hope to stay in Gwalior and study without a source of income? He had no answer to the question.

That evening, Pandey came over to his room unexpectedly and said, 'Come on, get ready. I have found a job for you.' Manoj could never have fathomed that Pandey would wipe out all his troubles in one go. Pandey's action was completely contrary to what Manoj had believed about him.

Riding their cycles, the two friends moved towards the PGV College lane, near Jeevajigunj. Once they reached a certain house, they got off and rested their cycles against its wall. The nameplate at the door read 'Rajneesh Tyagi'. Manoj immediately recalled that he was the man who had lectured at Vivekananda Kendra. Tyagiji had left a lasting impression on Manoj.

They went in and found him sitting on a bed, dressed in a white dhoti-kurta. Seeing them, he let out a thunderous laugh and said, 'Aha! Please come in. Haven't we met at the Vivekananda Kendra's Yuva Prerna Shivir?'

Manoj was pleased to know that Tyagiji remembered him. But it was more a vague recollection. He turned to Pandey and said, 'This young man is really bright. He was adjudged the best participant at the shivir.' The praise brought a smile to Manoj's face.

'Well, this is the bright young man is in need of a job,' said Pandey. 'His father is even fierier; he is busy changing the world. That is why he has no time for his family. Manoj comes from a family of fiery individuals,' he said, explaining the entire situation.

Tyagiji laughed and said, 'Pandey, you aren't any less fiery yourself.'

Manoj noticed that the air about Tyagiji was always cheerful and calm; his presence dispelled sadness and anxieties.

'It is hardly a job,' Tyagiji said. 'We need a caretaker for Sahitya Sabha's library at Daulatganj. Two hours in the morning, two in the evening. We will pay three hundred. If Manoj wants, he can stay in the library as well.'

The straw had rescued a drowning man; the proposal gave
a fresh lease of life to Manoj's ambition. Although the money
wasn't enough to rent a room at Peelikothi, yet he was happy that
he had found a foothold in Gwalior. It ensured that he need not
quit his dream and return to his village.

'How was your BA result?' asked Tyagiji, pulling him out of
his thoughts.

It was the perfect opportunity to impress Tyagiji and
he couldn't let it pass. 'It was good, sir,' Manoj said. 'I got
62 per cent.' In the excitement of it all, he had forgotten that he
had shared his real score with Pandey. And Pandey heard the
lie and was quick to intervene. 'Mr Manoj, as far as I remember,
you scored 55 per cent. Am I right?'

Manoj was caught off guard; he hadn't imagined that Pandey
would expose his lie. The revelation ruined the jovial atmosphere
in the room. Since he wasn't sure how to respond, he tried to
change the subject cleverly. 'I really liked your lecture on Swami
Vivekananda,' he said to Tyagiji.

But Pandey was bent upon laying bare the truth about
Manoj's result. 'Manojji, please leave Vivekananda aside for a
while. What was your percentage in graduation again?' Pandey
asked point blank.

In the past too Manoj had lied successfully to earn respect
from people. However, he was not so lucky today. He didn't have
the courage to look Pandey in the eye. Tyagiji understood that
Manoj had lied in a bid to make an impression on him. Before
things could worsen for Manoj, he decided to intervene and
diffuse the situation. Moreover, he found nothing too wrong
with it; he considered it a trait common to all underprivileged
village boys who came to the city, hoping to make a name
for themselves.

'I passed my MA English in the third division,' he said. 'Since people are not ready to believe it, I too have stopped owning up to it. In fact, some of my friends think that I have a PhD and they call me doctor. Truth be told, I don't even have an MPhil, let alone a PhD. But people have their own ideas and who am I to question them?' The trick worked; the tension was eased by his compassionate and jovial nature.

On his way back, an angry Manoj confronted Pandey and said, 'I had expected better of you; you humiliated me badly.'

Pandey reflected on the accusation and replied coolly, 'This was really necessary. Hereafter, your character and abilities will not be measured by a percentage. Instead of lying to bury your old weaknesses, you must face them with honesty.'

For a while, Manoj stared blankly at Pandey's face. Then the two set off in different directions.

18

Manoj had very few belongings—a bag, a bucket, a mattress and some books. He put everything on a tonga and set off for Sahitya Sabha Library. It was a century-old building and on the ground floor were a few timber shops. He could see a signboard that read 'Sahitya Sabha', on the first floor. He climbed up the winding stairs and found himself in an enormous hall packed on all sides with cupboards bursting with books. There was a small reading area in the middle. There was also a stage, not very large, but arranged neatly with a mike-fitted lectern to be utilized during literary events. The walls of the library were decorated with portraits of writers and other iconic people.

Manoj decided to put the stage to good use by laying out his mattress on it. Except during library hours, when a few readers came, he was usually all by himself. To fight his solitude, he took to reading books. He started with the biographies of legends like Abraham Lincoln, Thomas Edison and Tenzing Norgay—men who had braved adversities and prevailed. Lincoln's struggle with poverty left a deep impression on him, he became Manoj's hero. In fact, in order to look like Lincoln, he decided not to shave his thin beard.

The three-hundred rupee salary went entirely to a bhojanalay. He no longer needed to fret over lodging, food or books. The library hosted a poetry meet twice a month, bringing together some of the most well-known names in Gwalior. Discussions on social and literary issues were also routinely organized. During such gatherings, Manoj was in charge of the arrangements—from laying out the carpet to fixing the mike, he did everything himself.

He soon started taking great interest in the proceedings and dreamt of standing on the stage, and addressing the gathering or reading out his poems to them. Public speaking seemed most dazzling, almost divine, to him. At the end of each gathering, once everyone left, he would switch on the mike and air his views to an imaginary audience on the issues debated that day.

One evening, a poet stayed back in the library as his bus would leave only the next morning. He got up at dawn, took a bath and approached Manoj. 'Would you have hair oil?'

'No, sir,' replied Manoj.

Although the poet was a little disappointed, he decided to make another request. 'Doesn't matter, just get me a comb. I'll manage without oil.'

'I don't have a comb either, sir.'

'What sort of a boy are you? Alright, can you please get me a mirror? I'll at least take a look at my face before leaving.'

'I don't even have a mirror, sir,' replied Manoj, considerably embarrassed.

The poet was taken aback. At Manoj's age, boys obsess over their looks and fashion. 'Why have you taken to a life of severe austerity?' he asked. 'Boys your age behave like fashionistas.'

'I am preparing for the PSC exam, sir,' said Manoj. 'This job covers my expenses. But I don't see any need for hair oil or a comb. In fact, I haven't looked into a mirror for over a year.' His words conveyed a pride and dignity of their own. Since there was nothing more to say, he picked up the poet's bag and escorted him downstairs to an auto. While boarding the vehicle, the poet showered blessings on Manoj. 'Son, you will certainly succeed.' One could see a poem glitter in his moist eyes.

As he watched the auto depart with the poet, it struck Manoj that ever since he had shifted to the library, his friends had stopped visiting him. Pandey had also come over only once or twice during the past four months. He felt haunted by his loneliness and concluded that no one in Gwalior cared for him. The ghostly silence in the library tormented his soul. Only the lifeless books kept him company and he continued seeking them out.

One day, he picked up Maxim Gorky's *Mother*. Gorky's poignant portrayal of Pavel's mother and her spirited struggle against insurmountable odds moved him to tears. He could see his own mother's sad life mirrored in hers. In spite of all the adversities, his mother had encouraged him to stay put in Gwalior. Before he could finish reading the book, his own parents unexpectedly showed up at the library.

Seeing Manoj's miserable lifestyle, his mother could easily imagine the hardships her son had to brave. Overcome with affection, she caressed him lovingly. Since his father did not have much to say or to discover about his son's life in the city, he busied himself admiring the portraits on the wall. Most of the faces were unknown to him. Before Manoj could ask about his job and suspension, he pointed to a portrait and asked, 'Who is this man?'

'Muktibodh.'

'What do you mean?'

Manoj smiled and said, 'Muktibodh is his name. He is a poet. He has written many great poems."

'But I was fond of that Munshi. I remember reading his story in school … The one about the old Dukariya,' replied father, expressing his views on Premchand.

When Manoj's mother saw her husband engaged in useless chatter, she got angry and said, 'Do you see the life our son is leading here? Look how weak he has become. Please return to your job. The family debt is mounting fast too.'

His father did not take kindly to her interruption of his profound literary discourse. 'You illiterate woman,' he said rudely, 'you are such an ignorant. Look at these books here,' he snapped, trying to explain the importance of books to his simple-minded wife. 'There is so much to read and learn.'

An uneasy silence fell on the trio following this exchange. After a while, his father shared an update. 'The high court is my last hope; I am really counting on it to reinstate me. I have decided to fast unto death until they start an inquiry into the misdeeds of the deputy director.' It was clear that he was bent upon opening another battlefront in the administrative arena. But Manoj was more worried about his fast. 'Papa, please dump this idea,' he pleaded, trying unsuccessfully to dissuade his father. 'The court will reinstate you before long anyway. And don't worry about me; I am quite happy here.'

His father remained unmoved. 'I cannot rest in peace till I bring the deputy director to justice.' And having repeated his intention, he took up a seat on the stage and turned his attention to the grandeur of the hall. Perhaps the portraits of great men inspired him to carry on fighting. He straightened up pompously and got ready to make a speech. Addressing the large hall, the furniture, the portraits, the books, and his wife and son, he thundered, 'The greatest challenge our country faces today is corruption. People have become hopelessly self-centred. We are only worried about ourselves; no one is thinking about the nation.'

Before Manoj could speak, his mother jumped in saying bitterly, 'Don't you have any shame? You speak such nonsense; a man who cannot bring his house to order frets over the country! The boy hasn't got a new shirt in four years; we don't know where our next meal will come from. Mend your ways or it won't be long before we are ruined.'

Pained by his wife's reaction to his inspiring speech, his father said angrily, 'Stop wagging your tongue. Clothes make no difference to a man's character; an honest man will shine even in rags. And why fuss over food? Does that make us any different from animals who live to eat? A real man may starve, but keeps his soul intact. Do you have any clue about the challenges facing our country? Explaining these matters to you is like casting pearls before swine.'

'I may know nothing about the country, but there is something you don't know either,' retorted Manoj's mother.

'Oh, there is something that I don't know! Really?' His father feigned surprise.

'Yes. That you are a lunatic.'

Since it was time for them to return to the village, he ignored the observation and said, 'Shut up. You need to hurry or we will miss the bus.' Manoj escorted them downstairs. As they were waiting for an auto, his mother turned to her husband and said, 'Give him some money; your lecture won't satisfy his hunger.'

'I don't have any,' he said rudely and started looking the other away, in the direction from which the auto was expected to arrive. But his mother pressed a Rs 100 note into Manoj's palm and said softly, 'Son, take care.'

Once his parents left, Manoj returned to the solitude of his library. He settled down in a chair and wondered if his father had really gone mad. Could his mother be right about him? While he kept ranting about the nation, honesty, and the poor, he seemed least bothered about the problems at home. His mind, somewhat like a mad man, did seem to be fixated on these hobby horses of his for the last few years. Brooding over this issue, Manoj inadvertently picked up a poetry book lying nearby and started reading Muktibodh's '*Andhere Mein*' out loud. It was about an individual's obligations towards his country: 'What have you done thus far, how did you live your life?/ You've taken so much, returned nothing/ You've lived, the country is dying.'

His father's impassive face flashed before his eyes. He took out his diary and wrote, 'Indeed, those who worry about the nation instead of worrying about their families are branded mad. My mother is right; Papa has really gone mad. But I love my mad father. He is my hero.'

He felt lonely and sad. To lift his mood, he stepped out on to the balcony and stood there for a while, admiring the bustle on the road below. He thought of his village, how wonderful and joyous his village days had been. Ever since he came to Gwalior, he had forgotten all about his former self—the carefree easy-going Manoj.

A barat was merrily making its way down the road; it was the wedding season. The wedding party was grooving to a popular Hindi song—'*Mera piya ghar aya, O Ramji*'. Manoj noticed that the elderly revellers wanted the procession to hasten, but the younger ones, keen on dancing their way to the wedding venue, kept holding it back. Seeing the jubilant crowd, a thought came to Manoj—one must never be sad. Sources of joy lie scattered all around us. One has only to reach out and gather them. Times were indeed difficult for him, but he was firm on not abandoning his quest for a little joy. With that thought, he hurriedly shut the library doors and dashed downstairs in his slippers.

The band was still playing the same song, and the elderly were still in a hurry, frantically guiding the procession ahead. By the time Manoj arrived at the scene, the barat had moved a little further down the road. He made his way right to the middle of revelry and briskly requested the bandmaster to play '*Yeh kali kali ankein*'. Perhaps the bandmaster hadn't yet had the chance to put the full measure of his talent on display that evening, because as soon as the request was made, he started singing with gusto. The song electrified the younger members of the barat, whose spirits had been bogged down by the nagging oldies. Now, thanks to Manoj, the tables had turned and the assertive senior citizens were reduced to helpless bystanders.

Manoj danced his heart out. No one suspected that the energetic young man was an unsolicited guest. He danced for nearly fifteen minutes, till he was completely drenched in sweat. Then he stopped to catch his breath as the procession moved on.

19

A few days later, the manager of the library, Hukumchand, instructed Manoj to sell off all the scrap since the hall needed a fresh coat of paint. Manoj was quick to comply and traded everything for Rs 5,000. Later, when Hukumchand asked him for particulars, he also submitted the bills. Hukumchand stared at him with piercing eyes and said, 'Last year, we sold the scrap for seven thousand. How come we got only five thousand this year?'

The question was meant to cast aspersions on Manoj's honesty. Hukumchand seemed to insinuate that a boy who earned a mere Rs 300 would not mind stealing Rs 2,000.

'Sir, this is all the money we got,' replied Manoj. 'I reached out to seven scrap dealers and sold it to the highest bidder.'

But Hukumchand was not convinced and spoke, inflicting a deep emotional wound on Manoj, 'You are a young man and Tyagiji has such faith in you. You ought to have done better.'

Manoj had sworn to lead an honest life—a pledge dearer to him than all the charms of the world. But Hukumchand's accusation shattered his confidence. Bitterly angry, he wanted to offer a sharp retort. Instead, he quietly stepped out of the library, deciding not to work at a place that disregarded his honesty. But the very next moment, his mind was flooded by questions: Where should he go? Where would he live? How would he continue his studies? How would he support himself?

That evening, a listless Manoj sat glumly on a chair, holding a textbook of modern Indian history. However, troubled by Hukumchand's accusations, he felt no urge to study. Just then, he noticed his pitcher tremble a little. When he looked up at the ceiling fan, it too was swaying while rotating. The walls suddenly shook and he heard someone scream on the road: 'Earthquake! It's an earthquake!'

The old, dilapidated building shook for a few seconds. Thereafter, it grew quiet. Manoj rushed downstairs. By then, many shopkeepers had run to the open road in fear. They decided to wait there, fearing a recurrence. Mercifully, it didn't recur and people let out sighs of relief. However, someone in the crowd cautioned everybody that it might occur again later in the evening. Scared by the warning, Manoj felt hesitant to go back to the library. That evening, he loitered alone on the road till midnight.

After a while, tired of walking around aimlessly, he sat near a furniture shop, and started reflecting on his life. If the library was to come crashing down today, he thought, and I was to die trapped under the debris, would it have affected anyone at all? Who in the city would have come looking for me? No one! I have spent four years of my life wandering all over Gwalior. Have I got anything worthwhile? In spite of working honestly, I now stand accused of theft. What if I had died without the chance to wipe this blot off my name? I have surrendered my whole being to the PSC exam, but now even that appears so alien and distant.

He had been sitting for a while, but he did not feel like getting up. Manoj was now scared, sad and disheartened. There was no one he could share his sorrows with—his disappointments, the false accusation, an uncertain future and acute scarcity. He felt lost. By now, the road too wore a desolate look. He stood up distractedly and started walking towards the Ram Mandir

Chauraha. Since the temple gate was shut, he settled on the steps and started looking intently at the idol of Lord Ram, as if trying to have a conversation with Him. Perhaps he sought His aid in deciding the road ahead. Suddenly, he felt as if he had seen a gentle, reassuring smile flicker across His face. That night, Manoj sat there mesmerized, staring fixedly into the Lord's eyes for nearly thirty minutes.

Suddenly, a thought occurred to him: just like Lord Ram he too was out on a long journey. He too must face the perils that lurked on the road, and bear the torments that crossed his path. Talent did not bloom by itself, but flowered through untiring labour, limitless patience, total dedication, immense sacrifices and a burning desire for success. Buoyed by a strange energy that he felt coursing through his veins, Manoj rose to his feet and said aloud, 'I will not stomach false allegations; I will not let anyone put me down.'

With these words, he ran to the library, switched on the mike and started reciting a verse from Nirala's famous poem 'Ram ki Shakti Pooja.' As he read out loud, laying stress on every syllable, his voice quivered with excitement: 'Hain amaanisha/ Ugalta gagan, ghan andhkar/ Kho raha disha ka gyan/ Stabdh hai pawan char.'

'Ram seems to be on the verge of defeat. His world appears shrouded in darkness and disappointment. But the air of grimness cannot stub out the flame of hope that burns bright in his heart.' Manoj read out the explanation too and felt as if the lines described his own life.

20

The next morning he went to Tyagiji to announce his decision of quitting the library job. As soon as he reached his place, Manoj came straight to the point. 'I cannot work for the library; I don't want to be at a place that doesn't respect my honesty.'

Tyagiji let out his trademark laugh and offered him sweets, perhaps to defuse the situation. 'Since you don't drink tea, take this gajak.'

Once Manoj seemed at ease, Tyagiji resumed the conversation, 'Hukumchand is a businessman; he has put together his fortune bit by bit, selling hundred-rupee saris all his life. But while he knows everything about saris, he doesn't have the wisdom to judge a man. You are getting worked up quite unnecessarily. Go back to your work without a worry. I have complete faith in you.'

Reassured by the trust that Tyagiji had reposed in him, his confidence boosted, Manoj felt bold enough to stick to his point. 'Since Hukumchandji has lost faith in me, I can't bring myself to work for the library any more.'

Pandey and Anshu Gujjar, a former student of Tyagiji, walked in as he was speaking. Anshu was a talented PSC aspirant, all set to write the mains that year. Tyagiji decided to share Manoj's ordeal with them. But before Pandey could react to the story, Anshu turned and said, 'Tell me, Manoj, are you ambitious or not?'

Manoj replied instantly. 'I do wish to get selected in the PSC; yes, I am ambitious.'

'Then you must stay in the library. Your financial condition doesn't allow you to look for a new accommodation,' said Anshu, taking a pragmatic view of things.

But Manoj was firm about leaving the place. 'Didi, I can't be there; they doubt my honesty.'

'Then what is your plan? How do you hope to continue your studies without the job? The prelims exam isn't too far away,' added Pandey, munching on a gajak nonchalantly.

'I will quit my studies, live on the road, but I cannot compromise with my principles,' answered Manoj, without wasting a second to reflect.

Nobody knew how to counsel him, although they could see that his silly ideas and unreasonable idealism were borne out of his youthful vigour. Being a realist, Pandey had no patience with this extreme idealism. He turned to Tyagiji and said, 'Manoj is under the influence of his father. His father too refuses to compromise on principles. Not compromising is a family trait.'

Manoj had thought his pledge of honesty would impress these city-based intellectuals, but Pandey's cold and sarcastic observations disappointed him greatly.

Tyagiji picked up a book lying close at hand and passed it on to Manoj. The cover bore an image of Bhagat Singh. 'Tell me, Manoj, what is so special about this image of Bhagat Singh?' he asked. Manoj looked hard at the image, but could not offer an answer.

'I see restlessness in his eyes; I can see a yearning to serve the nation,' Tyagiji explained. After a brief pause, he added, 'I see the same restlessness, the same yearning, in your eyes too.'

Manoj was dumbfounded by this assessment; the comparison with Bhagat Singh was overwhelming. Anshu added her own words of praise. 'I too believe that Manoj's kind is very rare. I'm surprised to see that a boy his age can be so very faithful to his principles.'

At this point, Pandey turned to Anshu and said, 'Didi, yesterday at Tyagi Sir's school, a boy from class eleven wanted to read out his poem. It was quite bad.' He then looked at Tyagiji and asked, 'Sir, what was the poem like? Do you remember it?' But instead of waiting for a reply, he started reciting it from memory: 'Those who graze grass are better than me/ Those who carry a heavy load are better than me.'

'What do you mean?' asked Anshu, somewhat confused. No one could understand the context of Pandey's chatter.

'Yesterday, Tyagi Sir saw a bit of Jai Shankar Prasad in this great composition. I wish to tell Manoj that drawing parallels between average individuals and legends is one of Tyagi Sir's many hobbies. He ought not be convinced or moved by it. Instead, he should embrace truth and common sense.' Tyagiji himself could not help laughing at this analysis.

Though Pandey had cleverly dismissed the plaudits that Tyagi Sir had lavished on Manoj, he realized that someone like Pandey—who had never suffered poverty—could never empathize with him. He returned to the library, his mind still gripped by doubts.

A few weeks later, Pandey visited the library, but Manoj was not around. Hukumchand was seated on a chair, poring over the logbook. He told Pandey that Manoj had left the place nearly a month ago. 'Where did he go?' asked Pandey, surprised by this unforeseen development. Hukumchand did not speak a word but simply passed on a paper with Manoj's address on it—'Ghanshyam Flour Mill, Ganesh Mandir, Ghosipur'. Pandey went down the stairs looking at the note in his hand, and rode off on his bicycle towards Ghosipur.

Ghosipur was a densely populated slum in Gwalior. It had a narrow-gauge railway station that connected it to Joura and Salabhgadh. Pandey easily found the Ganesh temple. The place was dotted with heaps of garbage, and drain water overflowed the streets. He asked a local boy for directions and walked towards Ghanshyam Mill. He was sure that Manoj had rented a room at the mill owner's house. As he reached the mill, he saw a boy busily operating the grinder. Dressed in a white vest and red trousers, he was completely coated with flour. When Pandey approached the boy to ask about his friend, he had the shock of his life; it was Manoj himself!

Manoj smiled faintly at his friend and said, 'I'll be free in a while; we can then go to my room.'

Pandey waited at the mill, quietly observing his friend at work. Half an hour later, Manoj dusted himself clean, put on a shirt hung on a peg, locked the mill's door and walked with Pandey to his room. Pandey followed his friend silently, carting his bicycle along.

After walking for a while through the narrow lanes of Ghosipur, they stopped near a house. Pandey rested his cycle against a wall. They crossed a corridor and a courtyard to reach the farther end of the house, where Manoj unlocked the door of his room. Even though the sun shone brilliantly outside, the room was dark. Manoj had to switch on the light for Pandey to see anything within. A mattress lay on the floor. The shelves in the wall were packed with books. A stove and a few utensils lay in one corner of the room. There was a wooden stool on which Pandey decided to sit.

'I pay two hundred for this room, although it should not cost less than three hundred a month,' said Manoj. The house belongs to Ghanshyamji. He is a well-read man. When I told him about my problems, he agreed to lower the rent; he is a good man, and he likes me too. In fact, he has put me in charge of his flour mill. I work four to five hours a day and earn four hundred. That leaves me with enough time to study. I have come to realize that if one manages one's routine well, time is never scarce.' But as he spoke, he avoided looking Pandey in the eye. A boy who dreamt of staying at Peelikothi was now all praise for his new job and room.

Pandey heard him out attentively, but didn't utter a word. Suddenly, there was a power cut and the yellow light bulb went off. Once again, the room plunged into darkness. There were no windows to let in natural light. Although the door was already open, it was of little use; this part of the house did not receive any direct sunlight. Manoj lit a candle and waited for Pandey to speak.

'Manoj, you didn't listen to us after all.'

'I feel content because I chose to leave the library instead of abandoning my principles. Honesty must be preserved at all cost, even if it means suffering great hardship,' said Manoj, staring at the flame of the candle. Pandey could hear the sadness in his voice.

'But how do you propose to study for the PSC exam in this dark damp room?' he asked.

'The darkness in the room is not a problem,' replied Manoj. 'Trouble arises when we are lured by promises of comfort, and surrender our ideals and let our soul darken.' They could hear the noise of a train on the railway track outside. Pandey, a little thirsty, picked up a cup, poured a little water from an earthen pitcher and returned to the stool.

Soon they ran out of topics to discuss and Pandey took his leave. Manoj walked out with his friend to see him off. Pandey picked up his cycle and took a good, hard look at Manoj—his fair skin looked pale and yellowish, his eyes appeared sunken and he had grown a beard to hide his hollow cheeks. Instead of riding away at once, Pandey decided to walk till the end of the lane with his friend.

Once they reached the bend in the street, they stopped to say their goodbyes. 'Pandey, do keep coming. I felt so good today,' said Manoj.

But Pandey looked distracted; he was juggling a thought in his head. After a few seconds of uneasy silence, he looked at Manoj and said, 'I want to say something. Will you please hear me out?'

Assuming that Pandey wanted him to return to his previous job after seeing his pitiable living conditions, Manoj declared, 'I won't go back to the library at any cost.'

But Pandey was saying something else altogether. 'There is a place called Peelikothi near Harkishan Puram. The entire building is rented out to PSC aspirants. My friend Gupta stays there. Anshu Didi was also in touch with students who live there. Its ambience is perfect for studies. I'm planning to rent a room and stay there. If you agree to move in with me, it will be good for me. Will you?'

Manoj could not believe his ears! The world of PSC aspirants was really small and connected. For someone who had always longed to stay in Peelikothi, this was like a wish being granted. He had never thought that Pandey was capable of making such a generous offer. Given his circumstances, nothing better could have happened to him. But suddenly, his thoughts turned to his poverty. ' I don't have that kind of money,' he said to Pandey.

'Money assigned for one is always sufficient for two,' replied Pandey, mounting his bicycle. And then he left without waiting for a reply. Manoj stood there for a while, looking in the direction that Pandey had gone, swaying back and forth with happiness.

21

As decided, Pandey rented a room in Peelikothi and Manoj moved in with him, having brought all his belongings from Ghosipur. He soon found himself among students of the kind he always wanted to associate with; it was a bright and motivated study group. The prelims exam was close at hand. His previous attempt, taken immediately after graduation, had been unsuccessful. This time, he was determined to leave no stone unturned. He took out his diary and recorded his resolve: 'The atmosphere here is great for studies. I get to learn a lot in the company of the many brilliant aspirants who live here. There is no excuse for failure any more; I must work really hard.'

Meanwhile, Deep Soni had already appeared for the final interviews. One day, his father came over with the news that his son had been selected for the post of deputy superintendant of police (DSP). He spoke with tears of joy glinting in his eyes. 'I am a pensioner who earns only five thousand rupees a month. When my son started preparing for the PSC exam, everyone said it was an impossible dream; one needs to pay lakhs of rupees as bribe. But look what happened: he has now become a DSP, and we didn't have to spend a single penny.' So saying, Deep's father left to share the news with a relative of his.

'Bhaisahib, how do you feel today?' asked Manoj.

'Oh, I am thrilled,' answered Deep, his face beaming. 'But I must say something. I can guarantee that sooner or later, everyone who lives here will get selected.'

The residents of Peelikothi—Manish, Gupta, Pandey and Manoj—were delighted to have received such firm assurance. Manoj could see that those who eventually succeeded were no different. Deep's success had electrified the atmosphere in the building; the mood was festive. Soaked in joy and confidence, the boys stayed awake till late at night, talking about their future prospects.

Both Manoj and Pandey continued to toil relentlessly for the prelims exam. However three months later, when the results were declared, neither had qualified. Since Manoj had worked like a dog, giving his absolute best, he feared it was the end of the road for him. He fell into depression and spent the next few days in a state of shock, trying hard to identify his mistakes.

It was now clear to him that the road to the PSC wasn't as easy as he had imagined. He had no choice but to get over his failure and prepare for the next prelims exam.

22

Manoj's father was finally reinstated by the high court. After ages, his financial troubles had been finally reduced somewhat. That year, the PSC notification—usually issued in the month of November—got inexplicably delayed, triggering anxiety among aspirants. One day, the newspapers announced heartbreaking news: intent on reducing its expenditure, the state government had suspended the Madhya Pradesh PSC exams. The news spelt disaster for students across the state. A pall of gloom descended over Peelikothi too. Many sat dismayed in Manoj's room, brooding over the disastrous development and chalking out new strategies. 'Since the exam itself has been cancelled, does it matter however hard we study? I have decided that I will help my father run his transport business,' declared Manish.

'This time my preparation was so solid that no one could have stopped me from becoming a DSP, just like Deep Bhaisahib. But now that there is no exam, would there be a post in the offing for me?' whined Gupta. The grimness of the situation could not dissuade him from making too much of his abilities and even while lamenting, he did not forget to brag and exaggerate.

Pandey tried to inject a little optimism, and said, 'Where there is a will, there is a way. We should now try for the Uttar Pradesh and Rajasthan PCS exams.'

'You are so naive, Pandey. Students from other states never make it to UP or Rajasthan. If you are lucky enough to advance till the interviews, they will award a mere thirty out of two hundred just so you fail,' argued Gupta, rejecting Pandey's plan.

Even after hours of racking their brains, the boys could not agree on a course that had no unfair roadblocks strewn along it. Just then Anshu Gujjar reached Peelikothi. Like Deep, she too had become a DSP. However, she had kept up with the practice of visiting Peelikothi to help the young aspirants. Seeing their sullen faces, she put forth a new strategy and said, 'State service commissions have no future. You should now start preparing for the UPSC exams.'

The boys knew that the Delhi-based Union Public Service Commission conducted exams for the Indian Administrative, and Police Services (IAS and IPS) as well as other Central services. However, qualifying a national-level test was too sweet a dream for an aspirant of the Madhya Pradesh PSC. They feared that they lacked the calibre. To them, Anshu's proposal was not wedded to reality regarding their intelligence or their standard.

Clearing the UPSC exam was beyond even Gupta's wildest fantasy. He looked meekly at Anshu and said, 'Didi, it is too difficult. I don't think I can clear even the prelims. With hard work, we could have somehow made it to the state PSC, but getting through the UPSC exams is impossible.' Moments earlier, he had been raving about his preparation, but now his self-belief was beginning to ebb away.

'I am sure that if you spend two years in Delhi at a good coaching centre, it won't be all that difficult. After all, those who clear the exam do not tumble down from heaven. We must always aim high; we might miss the mark, but the flight will strengthen our wings,' said Anshu, trying hard to cheer the boys up.

Listening to her, Manoj felt his lost confidence return. 'Didi, this is not about getting a job; the dream is to prove one's worth.

We must keep marching down the road we have chosen for ourselves,' he declared. 'Either we perish or we prevail. We can't run away from the battleground. I will go to Delhi and prepare for the UPSC.' The spring that caused this sudden surge of strength, emboldening Manoj to make such an audacious public announcement, was a mystery.

Gupta tried to pull him down and said, 'A man who has never passed the state PSC prelims is boasting about clearing the UPSC. Huh! Mr Warrior, stop daydreaming. This is not meant for villagers like us who have studied in Hindi-medium government schools. How many from MLB College have become IAS officers? Those who make the cut come from places like the IITs, Delhi University or Allahabad University.'

Manoj drew in a deep breath and replied, 'Whatever be the case, we must at least try.'

Anshu too was firm on her stance. 'If it hasn't happened till now, it will hereafter; you will become the pioneers. Perhaps it is good that the PSC has been cancelled. Now you will step out of this little pond and swim the seven seas.'

'But how can Manoj go to Delhi? He barely scrapes a living in Gwalior,' interrupted Pandey, making Manoj's financial woes public. Reminded of his hardships, Manoj felt his wings had been suddenly clipped and he had crashed, falling headlong from the sky. Although his father had been reinstated, the deputy director continued to withhold his salary because of his refusal to go to Jhabua.

Seeing the sudden sadness wash over Manoj's face, Anshu asked, 'Are you really serious about going to Delhi?'

'Yes, Didi, I want to prepare hard, with all my strength,' answered Manoj.

'As they say, fortune favours the brave,' replied Anshu. 'I'll give you ten thousand to get into in a coaching centre.' Everyone was surprised by her generosity and Manoj was moved to tears. However, he was hesitant to accept the offer. 'Didi, I will raise the money somehow. But I'll always remain grateful for you kind thought.'

Seeing Manoj getting so emotional, Anshu rebuked him lovingly and said, 'Manoj, don't talk rubbish. You are like a younger brother to me, and I have complete faith in your abilities. You will definitely go to Delhi.'

From then on, Manoj started preparing for the UPSC prelims exam. After four months of rigorous study, he appeared for the exam in May.

'There is a five-month gap between the prelims and mains—a period extremely crucial for the aspirants. One can't afford to waste time waiting for the prelims' results. The ideal strategy is to start studying for the mains immediately after the prelims.' With these words of advice, Anshu gave him ten thousand to go to Delhi. That year, on account of fear and poor preparation, Pandey did not appear for the UPSC prelims exam. However, he too decided to join Manoj in Delhi.

23

The two friends reached Delhi, full of hopes and dreams. They got down at Nizamuddin Railway Station, took an auto till Kingsway Camp, and finally rode a cycle rickshaw to Mukherjee Nagar. They carried sacks crammed with books. They looked around with curiosity and excitement, marvelling at the numerous coaching-centre signboards that hung all over Mukherjee Nagar. The huge cut-outs, displaying pictures of successful candidates, filled them with awe.

Every student who comes to Mukherjee Nagar dreams of success and a billboard with their photo on it. But no one can tell who among the thousands will succeed, and who will fail. Each year, hardly 400–500 students taste success, as the UPSC announces only so many positions, while the aspirants number in lakhs. What happens to the rest? Having exhausted their attempts, many return home dejected.

But one can't give up hope simply because the number of failed candidates is frighteningly high; admitting defeat without struggle is cowardice. That is why each year, thousands flock to Mukherjee Nagar—setting aside fears of failure and defeat. It is not an ordinary locality, it is the karmbhoomi of India's intelligent, bright and optimistic youth—a pilgrimage for those preparing for competitive exams. Manoj felt a sacred reverence for the place.

He was also enthralled by the sights and sounds of the place. Tea sellers near coaching centres, juice shops teeming with young boys and girls, students flipping through magazines at book shops, a group fervently debating questions asked in the prelims exam, another passionate group discussing current affairs, a newly arrived student asking seniors for guidance—all of Mukherjee Nagar seemed completely immersed in studies, a sight that caused boundless joy in Manoj. He had never seen an ambience so vibrant. It made him regret the years he had spent in Gwalior. For the first time, he felt as if he had come to the right place.

Manoj and Pandey took up residence in C-block of Nehru Vihar, a locality adjacent to Mukherjee Nagar. Compared to Mukherjee Nagar, Nehru Vihar seemed like a lower middle-class colony. Its narrow lanes were dotted with closely packed multi-storeyed buildings. Since rents were relatively lower, those on a tight budget preferred this place.

Manoj was keen on taking classes for Hindi literature. When he asked around, he learnt that Vikas Divyakirti of Drishti Coaching Centre was the best teacher of the subject. He wasted no time taking admission. Since Pandey considered himself an expert in Hindi, he decided not to join. The institute operated out of a basement, right behind Batra Cinema. Miss Verma, the director, usually sat in her cabin. Next to her cabin was a huge lecture hall where Vikas Sir held his classes.

On his first day at Drishti, Manoj met a few students who had taken admission much before him. He could see aspirants from all parts of India in that group. Some of them had cleared their own state's PSC exam and were already appointed to prestigious positions, such as tehsildar and DSP. They were here in the hope of joining the IAS or the IPS. Others had previously appeared for the final interviews, some even twice or thrice. There was no dearth of aspirants who had cleared the prelims.

In Gwalior, it was very rare for someone to clear the prelims exam, but Mukherjee Nagar was swarming with those who had advanced as far as the interviews. Although Manoj was pleasantly surprised, he felt a little concerned too. Was he smart enough to compete against such brilliant students? He feared that he was no match for the scholars at Mukherjee Nagar. In a city that was crowded with successful students, he had come bearing the blot of being a twelfth fail. He wasn't sure whether he would measure up to the challenge.

It was already a month since Manoj had started attending Vikas Sir's lectures. There was a strange magnetism about his style of teaching and all the students were mesmerized. Vikas Sir had just announced that he would be conducting a test covering those portions of the syllabus that he had already taught. There was an air of excitement and anticipation in the classroom. At the end of the class, as Manoj emerged from the basement, he saw a group of students discussing the forthcoming test near a tea shop. He joined them instinctively.

One of the boys was all praise for Vikas Sir's judiciousness. 'If Vikas Sir approves of someone's answers, it is certain that the student will get selected. Last year, he spoke very highly of Deepender Kushwaha and he became an IAS officer.'

'In that case, this year, he will make a prediction about me,' bragged a boy named Sanjeev, sipping tea from his cup. 'I'll write such an answer on Jaishankar Prasad that he'll be completely floored. It will make him wonder from where this scholar has arrived.' To prove his point, he started reciting Prasad's 'Kamayani' from memory and would not stop until another boy in the group pleaded with him to conclude. Manoj barely remembered the first few lines of the poem and was enthralled by this spectacular display of memory.

A boy from eastern UP was also present. He started reminiscing about his time at Allahabad University and the brilliance of Sanjeev. 'People are entitled to their opinions, but I have known Sanjeevji ever since I was at the Tara Chand Hostel. He is a gold medallist in Hindi, that too from Allahabad University. My bet is on him; you can change my name if he doesn't top.'

'I think Rahul Rusiya will get the highest marks. He has been selected twice in the UP PCS—first in the department of trade and tax, and then as a DSP. On both occasions, his score in Hindi was through the roof.' Rusiya, who happened to be present, was overjoyed by the appreciation. He spread out his arms like the wings of an airplane, and embraced his ally. Finding himself stuck in the middle of such bigwigs Manoj freaked out; he stood no chance against such contenders. He wondered how many years of back-breaking study would make him as capable as these greats. Dejected, he slunk away to his room.

He knew that scoring well in Hindi was the key to getting selected in the mains and he really wanted to do well in the test. A good performance in the class test would mean that his preparation as well as his style of writing, both were on point. Once back in his room, he shared his concerns with Pandey. That self-proclaimed scholar of Hindi was ready with his penetrating insights. 'If you wish to do well in the test, your answer must be a class apart. Your language and your style, both should leave the examiner awestruck. Unless you manage to pull it off, he will neither consider you a scholar nor award you a high score.'

Producing some six books on Nirala—written by the likes of Ramvilas Sharma, Doodhnath Singh and Suryaprasad Dikshit—Pandey asked Manoj to read them all. 'Take these; they'll provide you a detailed analysis of Nirala's poetry.'

Manoj looked at the books and said, 'Of course, I'll read them; they are brilliantly written. But how does one produce a 600 word answer after reading a 200 page book?' Manoj wasn't sure which of the numerous ideas discussed in the books would make for a first-rate answer. Finding himself in a fix, he turned to Vikas Sir's class notes. Since he had attended all his lectures with great interest, it was easy for him to follow them. Each topic had been explained exhaustively, and his language was lucid too. Manoj decided that he would stick to the notes for the upcoming test.

The day after the test, Vikas Sir walked into the class and asked, 'Who is Manoj Kumar Sharma?'

Manoj raised his hand.

'This boy has the ability to clear the exam; he has secured the highest marks,' Vikas Sir announced.

Manoj could not believe his ears! How could he have possibly topped a class full of scholars? Did he really write the best answer? Was he really better than those who had already cleared state PCS exams? He felt like a hero, the subject of everyone's undivided adoration. It was a novel feeling. He had never witnessed a scene like this in his entire life.

Vikas Sir was a man of few words, known for his reticence. Today, however, he had been uncharacteristically effusive in his praise. As soon as Manoj stepped out of the class, he found himself mobbed by a group of girls. Perhaps, in him, they saw a future IAS officer. They had many questions too: How did you write such an impressive answer? Which books do you read? What is your native place? Which state PCS exam have you cracked? Between IAS and IPS, which one do you prefer? Have you appeared for the exam earlier too?

They fired the barrage at recently decorated Manoj at such a pace that he couldn't respond to any of the questions satisfactorily. By the time he could think of answering the first, a second question was ready. He had never imagined that within a month of his arrival, he would come to command such a fan following. Manoj stood surrounded by the girls, trying to soak in that warm feeling.

Just then, a sweet-voiced girl tried to draw his attention with an 'excuse me' and said, 'I am from Rajasthan. This year I cleared the state PCS exam and got appointed as an income tax inspector. However, I've come to Delhi hoping to become an IAS officer. If it's okay with you, let's go to the park and chat for a while?'

Before he could make up his mind, another girl asked and noted down his address, and said, 'I need you to teach me Premchand's *Kafan*. What is a good time to visit your room?' Manoj excused himself, offering only vague answers.

Another girl, who hadn't had the chance to ask a question, caught up with him and started walking alongside. 'Manoj, I have complete faith in your abilities; I am certain that you will get selected. How about we study together? Well, to tell you the truth, I like you a lot.'

Her forthrightness stunned Manoj. She wasn't the kind of girl who would waste time beating around the bush. He basked in the sudden stroke of luck, made possible by Vikas Sir's announcement. His long-standing wish to be called the best had finally come true. Although he declined her offer, he was thrilled by the events of the day.

As soon as he reached his room, he told Pandey all about his performance in the test and what followed. Pandey never expected him to do so well. He disinterestedly scanned through Manoj's answer script and nearly flung it on the bed. 'You are getting needlessly excited; this is an average answer. I see nothing special in it.' Pandey was, of course, green with jealousy. As someone who considered himself an expert on the subject, it was unacceptable that a novice had done so well.

Although Manoj was saddened by his friend's response, he did not protest. Instead, he started reading his answer all over again.

A few weeks later, the results of the prelims exam were declared. Manoj and Pandey rushed to a nearby cyber cafe. Manoj was quite nervous, his heart was pounding loudly in anticipation. Since Pandey hadn't appeared for the exam, he was unfazed. Manoj opened the UPSC webpage and could barely believe his eyes. He had cleared his life's very first prelims exams. Thrilled, he ran towards his coaching centre to share the news. A small group of successful aspirants had already assembled outside Drishti. Back in Gwalior, only one or two would manage to pass the exam. But here, nearly half of the students in his class had qualified.

He had, all this while, harboured the sweet illusion that qualifying in the prelims exam was an achievement in itself. But now reality struck him in the face—the prelims exam was nothing but a ticket to the mains.

As he stepped inside the class, he learnt that because of the results, the lecture would be delayed by fifteen minutes. He saw Verma Ma'am, the director of the coaching centre, sharing insights on Hindi literature with a girl.

'Have you studied Hindi literature earlier?' Verma Ma'am asked her.

'No, ma'am,' the girl replied.

When Verma Ma'am saw Manoj, she turned to the girl and said, 'Meet Manoj. He has topped the class test.' The girl cast a quick glance at him.

'You can talk to him about the classes. Within a month of joining us, his writing skill has improved remarkably,' added Ma'am.

'My name is Shraddha,' she said to Manoj. 'I'm from Almora and this is my first day in Delhi. Is this coaching any good? I've never studied Hindi literature. Do you think I can cover a subject totally new to me?' Her anxious eyes seemed full of questions and she was counting on a complete stranger for the answers. In her queries, Manoj could read an unsaid fear of a new subject. She was also keen to know more about Delhi.

Manoj could not take his eyes off this new girl—there was a mysterious charm about her that would not let him look away. At the same time, he felt as if he could see through to her soul; it was pure, transparent and did not conceal any secrets. Her radiant face betrayed all her emotions. She was sweet like a simple poem. Manoj stood transfixed, completely floored by her simplicity. Could this be that proverbial love at first sight? Manoj was baffled. He had lost his heart to her. In order to allay her worries, he praised Vikas Sir and said, 'He is a great teacher, particularly for those who are new to the subject. You have made the right decision.'

The class was about to begin and they sat together. Vikas Sir wanted to know how many had cleared the prelims exam. When asked, nearly half the class, including Manoj, raised their hand.

'Oh, you too?' asked Shraddha, a little surprised.

'Yes.'

'Which attempt?'

'First.'

Shraddha's Almora was no different from Manoj's Gwalior. In both the places it was rare that that anyone cleared the prelims exam. Naturally, she could not help idolizing someone who had qualified in his maiden attempt.

A few days later, Manoj went out to buy *Pratiyogita Darpan* from a book shop next to the Merathwala Restaurant, near Batra Cinema. It was another crowded evening at the eatery. Many students, free after long hours at their respective coaching centres, were greedily snacking. Others were enjoying their evening tea. A sweet voice greeted Manoj unexpectedly. 'Hello.'

It was Shraddha, attired in a sky-blue dress, her lips curved in a kind smile. Manoj's eyes were stuck on her face; his heart gladdened. 'Have you found a place to stay?' he asked, hoping to prolong their conversation.

'Yes, in Mukherjee Nagar. House number 1229,' answered Shraddha.

'And how is your preparation coming along?'

'Well, Hindi literature isn't as easy as people said it would be. I'm having a tough time.' She sounded a little low. To Manoj, that expression of sadness added to her innocence. Lost in its purity, Manoj started walking alongside her.

Shraddha's hostel was close to the culvert near Nehru Vihar. As they walked towards her hostel, down the quiet, dark road that connected Mukherjee Nagar to Nehru Vihar, Manoj tried to ease her anxiety. 'In the beginning, every new subject appears baffling. But within a few months, it will all make sense.'

'I don't know,' said Shraddha, still sounding doubtful.

And then they were quiet again. 'Tell me, have you heard about "Abu Khan's Goat",' asked Manoj, trying to end the silence. Shraddha couldn't make head or tail of this unexpected question.

'"Abu Khan's Goat" is a short story taught to students of class five in MP. Ever since I read it, I have imagined Almora as a picturesque hill station.' Manoj remembered that Shraddha was from Almora.

'Do you still remember that story?' asked Shraddha, surprised.

'Of course I do. A story about a city so very scenic is hard to forget,' replied Manoj, with a grin. Perhaps he hoped to win her over through flattery.

She laughed at his reply, which emboldened Manoj to ask more questions. He really wanted to know her better. 'Do you get snowfall in Almora? Is the weather so chilly all year round that you don't need a fan? How will you survive the heat in Delhi? Is walking through the hills really tiring? When your bus moves through the winding mountain roads, are you scared to look out of the window?' He kept asking questions without even pausing for her response. He had fallen head over heels both for Shraddha and her hometown.

His questions were quite intriguing. Shraddha wondered how a boy could imagine so much about a place he had never been to. Soon they reached the road that led to her hostel, but there was still some unfinished business; she had not yet answered all of Manoj's questions. 'Shall I walk you till your hostel?' he asked, desperate to spend a little more time with her.

Shraddha nodded. 'I really want to visit your beautiful hometown,' said Manoj, before leaving. However, he did not wait for Shraddha's reaction. Turning quickly, he walked away towards Nehru Vihar with hurried steps. That day, he felt a strange happiness of the kind he had never experienced earlier. Although Shraddha did not say much, he knew he had got his answers. He could read the empathy in her kind eyes. Soon he reached his room, but could not take his mind off her.

A few days later, as Manoj reached Drishti, he saw Shraddha administering first aid to a cleaner who worked there. The cleaner was sitting on a stool, grimacing in pain, while Shraddha was on her haunches, dressing his wound. A few students stood watching. One of them told Manoj that Shraddha saw Chotu's wounded leg, ran back to her hostel and brought ointment and bandage.

'Bhaiya, there is no need to worry,' she was reassuring Chotu. 'I'll change your bandage in a couple of days.' Then she looked up and saw Manoj, and a radiant smile lit up her face. For some reason though, seeing Shraddha lending a helping hand to a poor boy had caused Manoj's eyes to moisten. Shraddha was immediately concerned and wanted to know why he had teared up. But he did not answer her.

They walked into the class and, at the end of the day, decided to walk back together. Both of Shraddha's hands were occupied—she held the first-aid box in her right, and books in the left. Manoj relieved her of the first-aid box and said, 'Shraddha, you are very sensitive and kind.' He couldn't keep from praising her.

'Manoj, I am a doctor with a BAMS degree. This is my duty.' Manoj was reminded of his own bitter experience at a clinic in Gwalior. 'I have known doctors who have no qualms about throwing poor patients out because they cannot pay. The world's reserve of noble souls like you is fast depleting,' he told her. For Shraddha, the praise Manoj lavished on her was a great reward.

He told her about his experience at Dr Jain's clinic; she listened to him with great concern. Soon, they reached her hostel. Today, it was Shraddha's turn to wait at the gate and watch Manoj as he walked away towards Nehru Vihar. She sensed that there was another boy, full of untold stories, buried deep inside the very talented Manoj. She needed to know more about him.

Vikas Sir started a ten-day crash course for the Hindi essay paper. Pandey too joined this special module. However, instead of sitting next to him, Manoj sat with Shraddha. This irked Pandey greatly. He took a seat in a row behind them and sulked. Perhaps Pandey was upset simply because Manoj had befriended a pretty girl. Manoj noticed him staring and could feel the tension escalate. In a bid to placate Pandey, he introduced Shraddha to him and said, 'Pandeyji, meet Shraddha. She too has chosen Hindi for the mains. She holds a BAMS degree; I must say she is a very talented doctor indeed.'

But Pandey was not amused by the introduction. 'Manojji, there is no doubt Shraddha is brilliant,' he said loudly. 'But have you told her that you are a twelfth-fail aspirant?'

Manoj's heart skipped a beat. He had never expected Pandey to humiliate him in front of Shraddha. She turned to Manoj, perhaps for an answer. But he could not look her in the eye. He was hopelessly in love with her and wondered if she would break off their blossoming friendship.

Soon, the lecture started. Throughout the class, Shraddha sat with a solemn face. Manoj was beset with grave misgivings about their relationship; he feared that Shraddha would never reciprocate his feelings. The damage being done, Pandey was listening to the lecture on 'Economic development and the market' with total attention. At the end of the class, Shraddha asked Manoj, 'Can I speak to you for ten minutes?'

Manoj panicked, wondering what was on Shraddha's mind. Perhaps she wanted to tell him that she had no interest in a twelfth fail. It was only fair if she too wanted to befriend someone more likely to become an IAS officer. He walked on beside her, grappling with these disheartening questions.

Seeing them walkout together, Pandey called out to Manoj and said, 'Manoj, you have come to Delhi to study; put an immediate end to this premleela of yours. Have you forgotten why Anshu Didi gave you money?'

Manoj was extremely upset with Pandey, but reined in his anger and replied with calm civility. 'Pandey, she is a wonderful girl.' And then he returned to Shraddha, nearly sick with worry and ominous foreboding. As the two reached a juice shop, Shraddha asked, 'Is it true that you have failed class twelve? How come you cleared the prelims in the first attempt?'

Manoj could not answer. Although in the habit of lying to impress people, he could not bring himself to lie to Shraddha. He felt his breath stuck in his throat. What if she took him for a liar who had faked his prelims result? He decided to tell the truth. 'Yes, I failed because we could not cheat that year. Since I could cheat in class ten, I passed that exam with a third division.' A confidence born of honesty shone bright on his face.

For Manoj, Shraddha was already a part of his being. Could he hide anything from her? That day, they decided to sit for a while in the park near Shraddha's hostel. 'Manoj, I wrote the medical entrance examination twice, but could not make it to MBBS. And so I settled for a BAMS degree. I disappointed my father. Although I did work hard, success eluded me. I could never understand why! If I succeed in the UPSC exam, perhaps I can make it up to my father. But the feat that you have achieved is incredible! I feel so motivated listening to your story.'

Pandey's strategy had backfired; instead of severing her ties with Manoj, Shraddha felt all the more drawn to him. That day, Manoj sat with her for long, narrating stories from his village and Gwalior. Some of these saddened her, others tickled her into laughter. But mostly, she was amazed. As they sat gossiping, unmindful of time, evening darkened into night. Both of them wanted to forget about their past failures and look ahead to the promises that the future held.

24

The UPSC mains were now only ten days away. Manoj's preparation was far from thorough. Besides history and Hindi literature, there were two difficult general studies papers, for which he had not studied to his satisfaction. These papers would require him to answer questions on the Constitution, geography, the economy, science, current affairs and so on. He couldn't afford to take coaching in general studies and history. The English paper was compulsory and carried 300 marks. He drew comfort from the fact that marks obtained in English were not taken into account in the main examination. However, if one didn't secure the minimum qualifying mark of 100, all the other papers would not be even evaluated.

To cover the remaining portion of the Hindi syllabus, Vikas Sir took his last class at night. Manoj's coaching classes for Hindi were drawing to an end; now, he would have to go back to Gwalior. During the class, his mind was on Shraddha. He was not sure when he would get to see her next or whether he would see her again at all. Such a large world! Such long distances! Could a friendship of a few months blossom into a lifelong relationship? He couldn't tell. No matter how big the world was, or how long the distances, he wanted Shraddha to always be near him.

The class went on the entire night. Manoj stole a glance at Shraddha and kept imagining how pleasant it would be to remain in her company all the time. Vikas Sir concluded the class at

6 a.m. Manoj was now worried about his future. His mind began to wander. What would happen after he left Delhi? Would he see failure or success? Nothing was certain. Was it so easy to achieve success? To get through this tough examination? He was clueless. And what if he cracked it? Would everything fall into place then? He could then tell Shraddha that he loved her. But if he told her now, would she ever accept a loser like him?

When the class got over, he told her, 'Hang on a minute. I'll meet Vikas Sir and come back.'

Students had surrounded the teacher. On seeing Manoj, he gave his best wishes for the mains. Manoj touched his feet, stepped outside and found Shraddha sitting on a bench in the park. The pale sun was rising over the horizon. Its golden rays lit up her drowsy face.

'Shraddha, I'm leaving for Gwalior today in the evening,' he said. He wanted to say more, to pour his heart out, but his courage failed him. Wishing him the best of luck, she said, 'You are very hard-working. Leave no stone unturned in the mains. You will definitely succeed. If we ever meet again, I can proudly say that we were friends in Delhi.'

On hearing the last sentence, Manoj felt that she was leaving him forever. The prospect pained him deeply. 'Can't we remain friends?' he asked.

Shraddha thought for a while and answered, 'We are friends, Manoj. I don't know where I will go to pursue further studies. I don't know if my preparations for the civil services will lead to success. I also need to do an internship after completing my medical degree. Everything is so uncertain. Next month, I too shall leave Delhi. Most probably I'll complete the rest of my preparation at home.' Shraddha didn't want to lead him on. She was also not sure about how much and for how long she wanted to be friends with him.

Suddenly he felt as if she was drifting away from him. He didn't want her to go, but the journey through life is never a smooth one. It is a bumpy ride, fraught with difficulties and no dream can ever be fulfilled easily. Manoj had no idea where he would look for Shraddha once they parted. He asked her if she could share her phone number in Almora. Shraddha scribbled it down in his notebook. Human desires know no limits.

He longed to take Shraddha's hand in his. Could he do so without her consent? If only he could write his name on her delicate hands at the time of their parting. His wish remained buried inside his heart. He plucked up courage and said, 'Shraddha, my life has been a struggle. But I never gave up my dreams. Nor will I ever. I don't know why, but the very sight of you makes me hope that all my dreams will come true one day.'

Shraddha now had become an inseparable part of those dreams. But she didn't get carried away and responded to his emotional outburst with great poise. 'Manoj, I've learnt a lot from you about life. How to stay upbeat even after having failed the twelfth examination! When I see you, I feel inspired to study.' Manoj felt that she was the one with whom he could spend his entire life; the girl in whose company he could overcome any challenge.

An awkward silence followed. Looking intently at his copy of Jaishankar Prasad's *Kamayani*, he asked, 'Is this our last meeting?' He wished he could look deep into her mind. But is it possible to read a human mind?

'I don't know Manoj,' she replied, her voice tinged with sadness.

Would this memorable day with Shraddha ever return? Or would it only be part of his memory now? Manoj couldn't think straight. He remained tight-lipped as Shraddha walked away towards her hostel. He stood there, watching her with a sinking heart, until she was out of sight.

25

Manoj and Pandey boarded the general compartment of the Taj Express, their belongings stuffed into sacks. Manoj was returning with a heavy heart, his love for Shraddha etched on it forever. A thought crossed his mind: if only he could join the IAS or IPS in the very first attempt, he would be able to tell Shraddha that he loved her.

On reaching Gwalior, they rented a room in Peelikothi. Two days later, Manoj left for Bhopal to appear for the main exam. Deep Soni was posted there as a DSP and lived in a government accommodation. Manoj stayed with him. There was a ten-day gap between the general studies, compulsory English, and the other papers. So, he came back to Gwalior in the interim. In the general studies paper, his answers were far from satisfactory. Initially, he had fondly imagined that he would become an IAS officer, but now, he slightly lowered his expectations. However, there was still some hope that if he did well in the rest of the papers, perhaps landing a job in the income tax department or central excise department wouldn't be that difficult. Even a smaller post would do for now and he could aim higher in his next attempt.

A student called Avinash Mudgal had also rented a room in Peelikothi. He had only recently completed his BCom. Now as Avinash glanced through the question papers, Manoj said, 'I think I'll pass the compulsory English paper. I've written a terrific essay on "Terrorism in India".'

Avinash read through the questions once more and said, 'I don't see this topic anywhere.'

'Avinash bhai, you should read the questions carefully. Turn over the page and go to the third question. I've written at length about terrorism—its causes and impact on India, how to solve this menace, and the difference between terrorism in Kashmir and that in Punjab,' said Manoj, beaming with confidence, because he had indeed touched upon all these points in his answer.

Avinash was still struggling to spot the topic. When he gave up, Manoj took the paper and put his finger exactly where it was mentioned. 'Look, here it is. Can't you see this, Avinash?' he said in a rather annoyed tone.

Avinash exclaimed, 'Oh no, it's "Tourism in India"!'

Manoj turned his gaze on the paper; it was indeed tourism. How on earth had this happened? How could anyone commit such a goof-up! The answer about which he was so confident was incorrect. He had got confused between the spellings of terrorism and tourism. He felt as though his blood had frozen. Suddenly, everything went dark. None of his answer sheets would be evaluated if he failed to secure passing marks in this paper. How could he even dream of qualifying now! He had overcome the challenge of the prelims with great difficulty. All that hard work had now gone down the drain.

He fled to his room and burst into tears. English had undone him once again. The essay had been his only hope in the entire paper, and now he was going to get a big zero in it. The grammar-based questions had already stumped him, shattering his confidence. Eventually, he made up his mind not to go to Bhopal for the remaining papers of Hindi and history. Anyway, there was no point in taking the trouble if his answer sheets were to be left unchecked!

Thus, the first attempt was wasted because of his poor English and one dreadful mistake; it was an experiment that had gone terribly wrong. One year of hard work awaited him again. He would have to start from scratch. Days of sorrow stretched endlessly before him. How would he face Shraddha with this story of failure? He longed to see her again, to talk to her, but couldn't bring himself to do so.

Most of the students living in Peelikothi had appeared for the prelims of the Uttar Pradesh PSC. The results came out. Manoj along with Pandey, Avinash and Gupta had got through. Where the abysmal performance in the UPSC mains had dashed all his hopes, this success reinvigorated him—a thirsty man stranded in the desert had got a few drops of water to quench his raging thirst. Once again, he was ready to face the challenge of another main exam, even though it was at the state level. This bolstered his confidence and he felt an urge to call Shraddha. He was unable to forget her. Time and again, her memories came flooding back, tormenting his heart. 'No matter what, today I'll talk to her,' he thought. He rummaged through his room, but couldn't find her phone number. Dismayed, he sank into his bed.

'What are you looking for?' Pandey asked a disheartened Manoj. 'You have already wasted one exam. Now don't spoil another. The UP mains are round the corner. The clock is ticking. You better focus on your studies.'

Manoj was still lost. 'I can't find Shraddha's number,' he said. 'It's hard to resist the urge to speak to her.'

Closing the book, Pandey geared up for a chat. 'Please go ahead. Who has stopped you? But did it ever cross your mind what would you say? Hello, Shraddha! I've failed. After my twelfth exam, I failed in English again. Instead of tourism, I wrote an essay on terrorism. Call her. Let me also speak to her,' said Pandey.

Manoj's silence emboldened him further and Pandey continued to drop pearls of wisdom. 'Listen, Mr Manoj, girls don't like losers. If you want her, focus on studies. Get selected in the UP PSC. Then, perhaps she may fall for you. At the moment, all you will get from her are barbs and taunts. Be practical.' Like a self-styled guru, he had just delivered a long sermon on how to be successful in love.

Gupta and Avinash had entered the room while this sermon was ongoing. Since Avinash was not only the youngest among them but the brightest too, Pandey told him, 'Today, we will debate love. What do you have to say on this?' But Avinash had no interest in nonsensical chit-chat. He was a serious student who kept himself away from matters that could divert his attention from studies. 'Go and study, you scoundrels,' he scolded them, garbing it in jest. 'The UP mains are only six months away. Is this the time to fall in love?'

But Pandey was not about to give up so easily. As he persisted, Avinash said, 'What a waste of time! Love is like a leech. It clings to a student, sucking his blood when he needs to concentrate on his studies the most. Take my word for it, love-shub is utter nonsense. It's just the attraction to the opposite sex. Do you understand, Pandeyji? We get attracted to something that is beyond our reach.'

Manoj didn't quite like this nugget of wisdom. 'Love is the inner force that inspires me to study,' he protested.

Gupta ardently rooted for him. 'Wah, Manojji, wah! How aptly you have put it! Those would have been exactly my words too, but you've beaten me to it. Avinash knows nothing about love. He is a newbie! I wonder if he has ever lost his heart to someone!'

Avinash didn't find this amusing and said gravely, 'First get through the exam. You'll have all the time in the world to fall in love. It's difficult to be in love and succeed in life at the same time. It has a huge downside. Forget about everything else and focus on your studies. Don't keep the book open before you and daydream about your beloved. It will get you nowhere.'

Silence reigned in the room; everyone kept mum after listening to this piece of solemn advice, as they all had run out of ideas.

26

Manoj and Pandey took admission in an English coaching class run by Ravikant Dwivedi, an old friend of Manoj. English had undone him once. He couldn't afford another failure. Six girls and ten boys were already enrolled there. One day, Ravikant got angry and yelled at a girl called Yogita. Tears rolled down her cheeks in a flash. Pandey couldn't take his eyes off her exquisite face and declared her innocence in his heart, driven by the belief that a girl who sheds tears can never be at fault. He noticed that her dark eyes were bigger and prettier than those of other girls in the class.

Pandey, who was dead against Manoj's love for Shraddha, instantly fell for Yogita. The leech of love had latched on to him at such a crucial juncture when time was running out for the exam. Avinash was right about love after all.

Manoj heaved a sigh of relief, hoping that from now on his friend wouldn't mock his feelings for Shraddha. Pandey, on the other hand, didn't let any chance slip to befriend Yogita. In this, Manoj backed him firmly. But there was a catch. Persuading Yogita to reciprocate Pandey's sentiments would have taken ages, and they didn't have the time to waste on wooing her. So, they sprang into action and dropped by her house for a chat.

'Ravi Sir is full of praise for you,' Yogita told Manoj. 'He says you will definitely get through the PSC exam.' Manoj saw this as a golden chance for him to present Pandey as a worthy lover. He lost no time in saying, 'I'm not sure about my preparations, but

Pandey will certainly get through. His writing skills are excellent. In the college essay competition, he always stood first.'

Manoj had cooked up a white lie about his friend's exceptional abilities. It did have the desired effect of leaving a stamp of Pandey's personality on Yogita's heart. He came across as a good catch. Pandey, an idealist and stickler for the truth on other occasions, chose to keep quiet on this one.

With a broad smile on her face and a glint in her eye, Yogita cast a glance at him. Pandey sensed immediately that her heart had started beating for him. Never in his wildest dreams did he imagine that his persistence would pay off so soon and his love story would take off. Meanwhile, Yogita's mother brought a plate of poha for the lovers disguised as guests and left. A sudden silence fell over the room.

Manoj winked at his friend, so that he could carry forward the conversation with his new-found love. But Pandey was too busy munching poha. Manoj cleared his throat to drop another hint. Startled, Pandey blurted out, 'Your mother makes delicious poha. I have never ever tasted such a tasty dish. No one knows how to prepare this in our village. Manoj, you also tasted it first in Gwalior, didn't you? He he!' And he laughed and went back to eating.

Manoj let out a sigh of disappointment. Pandey treated everyone equally. Therefore, he talked to Yogita in the same way as he usually did to Avinash and Tyagiji. There was a guitar placed in a corner of Yogita's room and it caught Pandey's eye. 'Who plays the guitar?' he asked, while eating without a pause.

'I do! Who else will?' she replied, rolling her eyes.

'Music has a soothing effect on us. I'm not a good singer, but undoubtedly a good listener,' Pandey quipped.

Yogita liked his wit and said playfully, 'How will a good singer perform if there are no good listeners around?'

'Next time, when we come here, we'll definitely listen to your song,' replied Pandey. He stood up to leave and turned his unblinking eyes on her. A shy smile spread across her face, her eyes downcast. This was a broad hint that a new relationship was about to blossom. Music would give them an excuse to meet frequently.

With the seed of love sown in his heart, Pandey returned to his room. Books were scattered all over the place—some closed and some open. He found something distinctly odd about them. In the pursuit of love, he hadn't even cared to close the open ones. Presently, he kept them aside. As per the timetable pasted on the wall, both of them were supposed to read the chapter on the economic condition of India during the Mughal rule. Their fixed routine was already disturbed.

They both suddenly grew anxious about their studies. It was the month of December. The UPSC prelims would be held on the first Sunday in May, followed by UP PCS mains. Pandey peeped into the adjacent room and found Avinash completely engrossed in his book. A sudden pang of conscience for having frittered away their time spurred them into action. They decided to bury themselves in books.

After scanning through the pages for half an hour, Pandey's mind again began to wander as thoughts of Yogita came crowding in. Throwing the book aside, he lay sprawled, his eyes shut. Now, both the friends were on the same boat—torn between love and the exam. Pandey played a romantic song of a recently released film, *Mohabbatein*, on his music system. '*Soni, soni, ankhiyon wali*'. Soon, he was lost, daydreaming about Yogita's soni soni ankhiyan, her beautiful eyes.

27

Gupta had taken the two newbies in Peelikothi under his wing to help them crack the exam. 'Deep Soni and I had appeared for the interview together,' he boasted. 'It's just that luck didn't smile on me. I fell ill on the very day of the interview. Therefore, I didn't get good marks, or else, like Deep, I would have been a DSP today. Follow my advice,' he added. 'No force on earth can stop you from getting through the exam. Who do you think taught Deep how to write answers in the history paper? Of course I did. No wonder he scored well. Deep was like my student; can you believe it?'

The fledglings left the room in awe of the self-styled expert's Gupta's charismatic personality, crafted with lies and tall claims.

Avinash, accompanied by another newcomer, stepped into Gupta's room, followed by Pandey and Manoj. 'Guys, this is Naval Bhalla,' said Avinash. 'He will stay here.'

At the sight of another rookie, Gupta sprang into action. 'Excellent!' he said enthusiastically. 'Here, you will get a very conducive atmosphere for studying. Feel free to approach me whenever you have a query. I am known throughout Peelikothi for my expertise on international relations. Students come to me all the time. Don't they, Avinash?' Having considered Naval a greenhorn, Gupta had declared himself a subject expert and turned to Avinash, expecting him to endorse this claim.

Reluctant to contradict him, Avinash said, 'Gupta is quite famous not only in Peelikothi but also in the whole of Gwalior.'

Naval was anything but a greenhorn. Undaunted by the presence of these seasoned veterans, he made up his mind to test the depth of their knowledge. He pulled out his notes and threw a question at the group. 'Well, you all know about the recent visit of the Japanese premier to India. Tell me about the key points on which an agreement was signed between the two sides.'

The reputation of famed Peelikothi was at stake. The question flummoxed Gupta, who had bragged he was an expert on just this moments ago. He felt terribly hungry as soon as the question popped up, and edged away to the kitchen in order to put this time to good use. Four ghee-soaked chapattis and potato curry were heaped on his plate. There was an abundance of ghee for him as his family reared buffalos in the village. For the sake of courtesy, he offered food to the guests, but sensing his reluctance they felt too shy to accept it. Gupta couldn't make head or tail of the question and hence, went back to eating nonchalantly.

But Naval, not about to give up, prodded him again, 'Please tell me. It was an important visit. You must know this at least. Guptaji, you've a special interest in international relations. At least you should know the answer.'

Gupta was happily munching a piece of chapatti when Naval dared him to speak. With his eyes wide open, he forgot to chew and pretended instead to recall the answer. His acting was so good that it seemed the answer lay on the tip of his tongue, but he couldn't let it out because of the food stuck in his mouth.

Now it was the turn of Avinash, Manoj and Pandey to face the trial. 'What about you guys?' Naval asked.

No one knew the answer. Nor did they ever imagine that a newcomer would put them through such an ordeal. Naval was ruthless. Despite having beaten all the seasoned veterans, he didn't change the topic, though he took pity on them and simplified the question a bit. 'Okay, tell me at least the name of the Japanese Prime Minister.'

Naval thought that he had asked a very easy question, little realizing that it was no less difficult for them. All four continued to look dazed. Gupta again put his time to good use and scooted out of there to do the dishes. The other three conceded defeat.

Naval, who studied assiduously, as if he were preparing for war, had today—at the first opportunity—pounced on these students, treating them as enemies. He let out a sigh now that his foes were either massacred or writhing in agony on the battlefield. With a winning smile, he addressed his defeated opponents, 'You guys don't know even this much! His name is Junichiro Koizumi. He was wearing a blue coat and a red tie during his trip to India.'

Everyone was completely nonplussed by this answer. How could anyone observe so minutely! They found Naval intimidating. After this defeat, Manoj and Pandey were left with no option but to stare at each other. The next day, Naval returned with his luggage to stay in Peelikothi.

28

The excitement of the first day of the new year had unsettled Manoj a bit. After all, when would he speak to Shraddha if not today! New Year's Day was just an excuse, which he didn't want to miss out. Manoj shared his dilemma with Pandey, who empathized with him and offered to help as he himself was besotted with Yogita. Manoj hunted through the entire room to find Shraddha's number but to no avail. Yogita's love had turned the hard-hearted Pandey into a kind-hearted person. 'Don't lose hope,' he said softly. 'Keep on looking. You'll definitely get her number.'

After digging through all the papers for another fifteen minutes or so, Manoj felt disheartened. A generous Pandey didn't like to see his friend feeling so miserable. His fertile mind came up with an idea: 'We can get her number from Vikas Sir's coaching centre.'

The proposal filled Manoj with fresh energy. They went straight to a nearby telephone booth with the phone number of Drishti Coaching Centre. Verma Ma'am, the director, knew Manoj well. He dialled her number in the belief that he would easily get Shraddha's number.

'Namaskar, this is Drishti Coaching! How may I help you?' the lady said.

'Namaskar, Ma'am! This is Manoj calling from Gwalior,' he said confidently. 'I've attended classes in your centre. My friend Shraddha also studied there. May I get her phone number?'

The lady remained unmoved by this introduction. Her reply was curt. 'No, sir. We can't give you anyone's number.'

'Perhaps she couldn't recognize me,' thought Manoj, and tried to remind her. 'This is Verma Ma'am, right? I am Manoj from Gwalior.'

'Ma'am is on leave. And you are talking to Rakhi,' she said gruffly.

But this was his last hope. So, he didn't give up and said, 'Ma'am, you don't get it. It's urgent. Her form for the IAS exam has been cancelled. I need to speak to her in this regard.' Such fibs were his time-tested weapons, and had come to his rescue on numerous occasions. But this time, the lie failed to hit the target. The lady, who must be used to getting all sorts of calls, hung up on him abruptly.

Angry, Manoj called up again in the hope that he could talk to Vikas Sir directly. After all, Sir was always full of praise for him, and certainly wouldn't disappoint him. 'I need to speak to Vikas Sir. I'm his student and have written the UPSC mains,' he said, assuming that this would make an impression on her and she would put him through. 'He has taken time off for a trip to Rajasthan,' came the response.

Manoj's last hope was also dashed and he was back to square one. Try as he might, he couldn't find a solution to the problem. His face fell. Pandey noticed this and felt equally disappointed. Determined to help his friend reach his destination in love, he hit upon an idea. 'Manoj, all your options are exhausted now. You must go to Almora. Without baring your soul to Shraddha, you won't be able to have peace of mind.'

The distance from Gwalior to Almora is about a 1,000 kilometres. Manoj wondered how he would get there. And if somehow he did, how would he meet Shraddha? Could he walk into her house straightaway? No, her parents would be there.

What would he tell Shraddha? Why had he come? To get her phone number? Manoj asked himself.

Finally, he said, 'Pandey, it's not so easy to travel all the way to Almora. That's quite a distance.' The thought of visiting such a far-off place unnerved him.

'First catch a train for Delhi, then take a bus from there. It's very simple.' Pandey was enthused, but Manoj was still in a fix.

'What doesn't love make one do!' continued Pandey, prodding him into action. 'With one leap, lovers cross mountains, rivers, streams and what not. And look at you. Can't you travel even to Almora? How far is it anyway? Start now and by morning you will get there.'

Smitten with Yogita, Pandey could empathize with a fellow lover's agony and was quite eager to lend a helping hand. Manoj acted on Pandey's generous advice and planned to set off for Almora. Some notes of Hindi literature were lying with Pandey. He handed them over to Manoj like a weapon supplied to a soldier about to enter hostile territory. 'Keep them. They will come in handy when you get into Shraddha's house.'

Manoj already had saved up some money. This, along with the Rs 500 that Pandey gave him, would take care of the travel expenses. Pandey saw Manoj off at the railway station. And then he made his way to a phone booth, called up Yogita and spent hours chatting with her, giggling intermittently.

29

On reaching Delhi, Manoj caught a bus owned by Hina Travels from the Anand Vihar terminal for Almora. He had always wished to see the breathtaking scenery of the hills, but today, he felt quite jittery. His mind began to wander. All night, he kept on imagining how he would meet Shraddha. How would she react if he suddenly popped up at her house? What excuse would he make before her parents? These questions completely bewildered him.

Dawn was now breaking over the valley. Towering mountains cloaked in mist stood all around him with clouds as fluffy as white cotton balls floating over them. It felt as though he could touch them by stretching his hands out through the window of the bus. The picturesque view of the mountains mesmerized him. 'Perhaps Shraddha looks so innocent and ravishing because of being born and raised in this pristine environment,' he thought to himself.

Having reached Almora, Manoj freshened up in a cheap lodge and stepped outside with an envelope of notes that Pandey had given him. Shraddha had narrated plenty of stories about her hometown and about Mall Road. Below Mall Road stood Sarvodaya Nagar. She lived some fifty flights of steps down this colony. Today, Manoj was on the same stairway that Shraddha climbed daily. These steps made him feel her presence. But as he climbed down, his confidence weakened with each step.

Within minutes, Manoj had arrived in front of a mansion. The nameplate read 'Professor Ganeshchandra Joshi'. His mind went blank; his fertile imagination seemed to have deserted him. How would he face Shraddha? What would he tell her? Steeling his nerves, he rang the doorbell and held his breath. His heart pounded and his legs shook. Does everyone feel the same on visiting their beloved's house for the first time? This was a new experience for him. Meanwhile, a young boy, who looked like a servant, stepped out. Manoj cleared his throat and said, 'I've come from Delhi to meet Shraddha Joshi.'

The boy asked Manoj to follow him. Now, Manoj was entering the house where Shraddha lived, passing through the garden where roses, marigolds, chrysanthemums, and each and every flower had bloomed thanks to her delicate touch. The boy made him sit in the drawing room and went inside. In the glass-fronted cabinet sat several trophies and cups won in debates, essay-writing competitions and music contests. The name Shraddha Joshi was etched on each of them. On the wall hung a picture of Shraddha drawing a rangoli.

Manoj waited for her with bated breath—his eyes, face and mind beyond his control, ready to give away his secret. His ears longed to hear her melodious voice and his eyes grew restless to see her exquisite face. At this point, Shraddha's mother walked into the room. Manoj greeted her reverentially and said, 'Auntie, Shraddha and I studied together in Delhi.'

She hadn't called out for Shraddha yet. She might want to test Manoj first to make sure that he was not some shady guy. Or who knows, like Morena, in Almora too there could be a custom of not letting one's daughter meet a stranger, particularly a boy. It was also quite possible that Shraddha had gone out somewhere. All sorts of questions and misgivings crowded his mind.

'Are you from Delhi?' asked Shraddha's mother.

'No, I'm from Gwalior.'

Manoj was reluctant to chat with the mother for long, but she seemed to have all the time in the world to grill him.

She said, 'I've heard a lot about Gwalior, Bhind and Morena.'

He drew great comfort from the fact that his town was pretty famous even in the far-flung mountains. But, to his dismay, her mother asked, 'Do you get to see robbers brandishing guns even these days? I've heard people over there are quite quarrelsome, ready to shoot each other at the slightest of provocation.' This music teacher was taking a keen interest in sociology.

The discussion seemed to pose a grave threat to Manoj's future. It was hard for him to imagine how the guns of Chambal, without even being fired, had struck terror in a place as far-off as Almora. However, he tried to handle the situation with care, saying amiably, 'Things have changed now. Gwalior has, of late, made impressive strides in improving the education sector.'

Shraddha's mother chatted about everything under the sun except her daughter. He stood hesitating over how to ask her to call Shraddha. Pulling out Pandey's notes from the envelope, he said, 'Auntie, I have got these for Shraddha.'

Finally, the mother revealed the secret. 'Oh, I forgot to tell you she has gone off to Haridwar for an internship. Give the notes to me. I'll pass them on to her.'

The castle that Manoj had built in the air came crashing down. But it was not in his nature to yield so easily. He mustered the courage to ask, 'Can I have Shraddha's number? I seem to have lost it.' For a moment, he stopped worrying about what her mother would think of him. Much to his surprise, she turned out to be quite generous and gave him the phone number of Shraddha's hostel.

On returning to the bus stop, he decided to call Shraddha before saying goodbye to the town. He dialled the number. The phone began to ring. He could feel the thud of his heartbeat. If he didn't talk to her, he grew restless; and when he got a chance to do so, he felt equally restless. His racing heart was beyond his control. He kept on waiting, the phone kept on ringing.

Eventually, a lady picked it up. 'I am calling from Almora. May I speak to Shraddha Joshi, please?' asked Manoj.

'Hang on, she will be here in a moment,' replied the lady.

In a short while, Shraddha was on the call. The time had come for Manoj to listen to the voice he had craved for so long. 'Hello!' said Shraddha softly.

'Her deep, velvety voice was as bracing as fresh air, as invigorating as the herb sanjeevani,' thought Manoj to himself. Wasn't it the most mellifluous voice of the world? Wasn't he dying to listen to her!

But he couldn't bring himself to utter a word.

'Hello, who is this?' Shraddha asked again.

'This is Manoj speaking.' He finally broke the silence.

'Manoj, you?' Shraddha recognized him. The time for fantasy was over as he was brought back to reality.

'Are you calling from Almora?' she asked, gasping in wonder.

'Yes, I am,' replied Manoj, as if in a trance.

'Why have you come to Almora?'

'To meet you.' Manoj couldn't tell her a lie.

'Did you go to my house?' Shraddha asked, her voice firm.

It didn't take her long to figure out that Manoj managed somehow to procure her phone number from her house. 'You have travelled all the way from Gwalior to Almora only to meet me. May I ask why?' She sounded as though uncomfortable with Manoj's impetuosity, as she indeed was.

'Had she completely forgotten the time they spent in Delhi?' wondered Manoj. 'Do girls forget everything so quickly? Do they have such weak memory or they just pretend?' He was baffled by her behaviour. But he remembered everything, each and every moment spent with her. His eyes shut and his voice shaking, he confessed to her: 'I can't live without you, Shraddha. I'm dying to meet you, to talk to you.'

'Have you lost your mind? You are insane. I thought you were a sensible guy. Don't ever call me,' she thundered and slammed the phone down. Each word burnt Manoj's heart like a flash of lightning. Her voice had given way to the irritating bleep of the telephone.

It dawned upon him that the path to success in love was not as smooth as he believed. He had just had his first exposure to the other side of love, which was harsh and suffocating. Tears slowly rolled down his cheeks, making the telephone wet. With a crestfallen face, he sat at the bus stop right outside the telephone booth. Little had he expected such harsh behaviour from Shraddha. Was there really no place for him in her heart? Was it all merely fantasy? He continued sitting silently for a while, and then suddenly her face flashed through his mind. 'No,' he thought. 'I can commit a mistake in understanding anyone else, but not Shraddha. She is the best; she can never be wrong. It's my fault that I went to her house. I shouldn't have come to Almora.'

A moment ago, Shraddha's stern rebuke had unsettled him. However, he didn't let this affect his estimation of her. The love and trust he had felt for her remained undiminished. Just then, the booth operator called out his name. 'Are you Manoj Sharma? There is a call for you.' Manoj hurried to the booth and found Shraddha at the other end.

Concealing her anger, she said, 'Do you have any idea what you are doing? At this stage, studies should be your top priority. By the way, how did you fare in your mains?'

A young man, who had covered a distance of more than a thousand kilometres in the pursuit of love, was asked to produce a report card of his studies. His life was already a long series of failures. One more feather had been added to his cap when he dropped out of the mains exam midway, committing a blunder in the English paper. Shraddha was asking him about that very achievement.

'I opted out of the exam. Somehow wrote the essay on a wrong topic.' After a moment's hesitation, he narrated at length how he had messed up the paper.

Shraddha took a long pause and exhorted him, 'At this juncture, except your career nothing else should come into your mind. One hardly gets a chance to write the mains and you left it midway. And instead of overcoming your weakness, you are loafing around in Almora, talking nonsense. Tell me, will you ever succeed in life if you continue to act so casually?'

Speechless, Manoj listened to her with rapt attention. His heavy heart became light again. He was not fearful or apprehensive any more. Neither about Shraddha, nor about his future.

30

Manoj's quest for love remained incomplete, but Shraddha's kind words and practical advice gave him the nudge he needed. With the message of his beloved etched in his memory, he returned to Gwalior. It was his second attempt at the prelims exam, which was only three months away.

He penned down in his diary: 'I'll never disappoint you. You are the one who showed me the right path. Had I not gone to Almora, perhaps I would have continued to be on the wrong track. Now I must sweat and swot day and night.'

It was 11 a.m., and Manoj and Pandey decided to read seven to eight hours at a stretch. In the next room, Avinash, Naval and Gupta had their heads buried in books. Yogita had just called up the telephone booth on the ground floor of Peelikothi, to say that she was coming over. Pandey grew restless and dropped the idea of studying. Although the history book lay open in front of him, his mind was far away. Time went by; morning gave way to afternoon. Pandey got fidgety, but Yogita didn't show up. Neither could he read a word. One moment, he was on the roof; the next, downstairs in his room. He wandered all around Peelikothi like a ghost, desperately waiting for Yogita.

In order to kill time until she arrived, he peeped into Naval's room and found him immersed in study. Naval looked up and went back to reading without even nodding his head in greeting, making it amply clear that he didn't want to be disturbed. Seeing his blank expression, Pandey realized that his presence was not welcome and left right away, unleashing a torrent of abuse at him in his thoughts.

Yogita finally showed up at around 5 p.m. and an anxious Pandey heaved a sigh of relief.

'Sorry, I got a little late. My elder sister is getting married on the twentieth of this month. You all are invited. Do come,' she said, her eyes twinkling. Having waited for five long hours, Pandey managed to be with her only for five minutes. Once she left, he sprawled out on the bed. As all his anxieties were put to rest, his thoughts returned to reading and he flipped a book open, feeling quite upbeat.

After skimming through the pages for ten minutes or so, his eyes fell on the invitation card Yogita had given. He fixed his steady gaze on it and then, suddenly possessed by a strong urge to listen to music, played his favourite song from the film *Mohabbatein* at full volume. Naval couldn't stand it, so he burst in and asked him to lower the volume. Manoj did so on Pandey's behalf and Naval went back to his room.

Pandey was a bit miffed about this intrusion. 'Naval pretends to read all the time. Don't we study? We never get distracted by music. On the contrary, we can concentrate even more,' he said and showered Naval with a stream of abuse.

31

Meanwhile Manoj had run out of money. When he got to know that his father had come to the village, he set out home to meet him and collect money for further studies. As soon as he got down the bus, he ran into Vishnu and Balle, his old friends, on the culvert. Vishnu had become a teacher in a government school. 'So, Manoj, you are back? When will you become a deputy collector? It has been several years now since you left,' he scoffed.

Little did Manoj expect that he would have to face such barbs as soon as he had entered his village. However, he responded calmly. 'It'll be done, Vishnu. These things take time.'

Vishnu was well aware of the standard of his old twelfth fail friend. He suspected that Manoj just loafed around in Gwalior and had fun, swayed by the ways of the city. 'You can't befool me. I know you and also what all you read.' Vishnu had no faith in his friend's abilities.

Balle had stopped driving the tempo and had started doing construction work in Joura. 'Why have you shaved off your moustache?' he asked. 'Wearing spectacles too, eh? These are not good signs. I think you have trapped some girl in Gwalior. Bhaiya, don't bring a bad name to our village.'

Having listened to these barbs and jibes from his friends, Manoj felt somewhat humiliated and headed home. His father was seated on the veranda, poring over some documents. Kamlesh was not home and his mother had gone to the neighbour's house for a chat. Rajni was busy doing household chores.

As soon as Manoj stepped into his house, he realized that Shraddha was way beyond his reach. He had seen her mansion, as well as her picturesque town. How tiny and deprived his village was compared to Almora. No one had even the most basic etiquette in his village. Everyone spoke rudely, everyone used barbs and taunts. What a palatial house Shraddha owned, and how cramped his place was! Finally, it dawned upon him how unrealistic his expectations were to have a lifelong companionship with Shraddha. She was way out of his league.

On noticing Manoj, his father roared, 'Huh! When did you come?'

Without waiting for his son's reply, he began narrating his story. 'Now they want to transfer me. Let me also see how much guts they have! I'll teach them a lesson. What does the deputy director think of himself! Bloody scoundrel!'

For the last one year, his father's job had been in a mess, but once again, he was bracing himself for another prolonged fight with his superiors and had started sharpening his rusty weapons after taking a break. Manoj sensed that he could be suspended at any moment. For the first time in his life, he entreated his father to manage the household finances. 'Papa, please have patience for a couple of years and don't pick up a fight with anyone in your office. I've to go to Delhi to join coaching classes. For that I'll need money.'

The father turned a deaf ear and said, 'You don't know these guys well. Bastards they are. All of them. I'll certainly teach them a lesson.'

It became fairly clear to Manoj that his father's actions would bring him into direct confrontation with the authorities and then there would be no stopping him. The crisis was going to deepen and the tension was sure to escalate. Any day, the bad news could come in that he had been suspended. On the other hand, it was impossible to do well in the mains without getting into a proper coaching centre in Delhi. Qualifying in the prelims was possible even by staying in Gwalior, but Delhi was a must for the mains.

The next day, having got Rs 2,000 from his mother, Manoj set out for Gwalior. On the way, he kept thinking that it was pointless to dream big, to think of the IAS, IPS, and Shraddha. He had come to his village with a lot of hope, but was returning in despair.

32

Pandey and Manoj were all set to attend Yogita's sister's wedding. Avinash owned a red Maruti car. Pandey invited him to come along, because he wanted to create a good impression on his girlfriend by going to her house in a car. In return for the delicious food of the feast, Avinash readily agreed. On reaching the wedding venue, Pandey was delighted to see Yogita all dolled up for the occasion. With a great sense of pride in his choice, he nudged Avinash and said, 'Look at her! Oh, she is beautiful as hell!'

Avinash had come to the party with a clear objective. He had no interest in such nonsensical talk. Without wasting even a fraction of a second, he heaped a mountain of food on his plate and began gorging on it. 'Pandey, matar paneer is delicious. You should try it. You are just wasting your time. Don't forget, we have to go back and study,' he said. But on this romantic occasion, Pandey's hunger and thirst had already died, and as for the exam, it was the last thing on his mind. He turned his gaze on Yogita, who was smiling while talking to the guests chirpily. 'Look, how happy she is!' said Pandey.

'She is overflowing with happiness because you are here,' said Manoj, to his friend's satisfaction.

Avinash hadn't had dahi vada for many days. While eating it slowly and with relish, he said, 'Pandey, the dahi vada is yummy. Do you want to try it?'

Pandey was still lost in Yogita's beauty. Miffed by the distraction, he growled, 'Go and stuff yourself first.'

On the other hand the festivities were bringing back memories of Shraddha to Manoj, making him feel miserable. So, now there was a strange situation: one lover longed for his lady love living in a far-off place, and the other feasted his eyes on his beloved, who stood within his reach.

'You are right, Manoj. Yogita seems to be excited to see me,' said Pandey, letting out a deep sigh of contentment.

Avinash wanted to laugh heartily at Pandey, but remained silent fearing that the kadi chawal that he was eating with gusto, might spill over. However, once he was done with it he spoke his mind bluntly. 'Pandey, are you stupid?'

'You always talk rubbish, Avinash,' snapped Pandey. 'What do you know about the pleasure of being in love? It was a big mistake to invite you. What do you have to say anyhow?'

Sharp-eyed Avinash drew his attention to something that blinded-in-love Pandey was unable to see. Enjoying gulab jamun dripping with syrup, he said, 'You are not the reason for her happiness. Look at her carefully. There is a guy taller and smarter than you, clad in a black coat. She is in high spirits because of him. Can't you see?' Though Avinash had come along uninvited and only to eat, he fulfilled the duties of a friend by bringing Pandey back to reality.

Pandey and Manoj turned their eyes to Yogita and found her laughing and talking to a spruce and handsome young man. Even after seeing this, the starry-eyed lover continued to oppose Avinash and rebuked him. 'You derive pleasure from the problems of others. Yogita has got many guests here and it is the sacred duty of a host to entertain her guests.'

'It's fine if you don't admit it. But I am dead sure Yogita is into that boy. You are unnecessarily being a spoilsport between them,' said Avinash confidently.

Pandey now became alert to the danger. He had never imagined that another man could bring her happiness. While sipping coffee, Avinash gave his final verdict. 'You are not needed here any more. Your Yogita has already found a more suitable and handsome boy for herself. Let us go, and you better return to your studies.'

Pandey seemed unnerved. 'I don't believe you. Let me go and find out on my own,' he said fretfully.

'You just wait and stay calm. I'll discover the truth,' said Manoj, trying to pacify a flustered Pandey.

With a nod and a smile, Manoj approached Yogita and said, in order to test her, 'So, we'll take your leave.'

Before she could respond, he shook hands with the tall, dark and handsome man, and said, 'Hello! I am Manoj.'

'Shashank,' the young man amicably answered.

Yogita said, 'Shashank is my brother-in-law's relative. He works as a software engineer in England.'

The introduction was short and kind of incomplete, but enough to strike fear in the heart of Pandey who was within earshot. He realized right away that he was nothing before that engineer. His face turned pale in the bright lighting and glare of the party. The fear of defeat suddenly loomed large, and he felt utterly devastated. The dashing man, on the other hand, sought their leave. Manoj was determined to discover the whole truth about him. So he said, 'Yogita, Shashank is a nice guy.'

It didn't take her even half a second to get what Manoj implied. She eagerly asked, 'Really?'

To enquire further, Manoj said, 'Don't forget your old friends once you settle down in England.'

Yogita went all shy and nodded to the effect that after going to England she would not forget her friends. It was of little importance to Pandey now whether Yogita would remember him or not. They all stood in silence for a while. Pandey averted his eyes from Yogita's face. 'You guys shouldn't leave without having dinner,' said Yogita to Manoj. She sighted Pandey and edged away to the other side. On noticing that there was no one else with his friends, Avinash strode across to them.

'You were spot on, Avinash. Yogita is in love with that Englandwallah boy,' said Manoj.

Avinash continued to speak in the same scathing tone he had used earlier. 'Pandey, should we leave or would you like to eat? The girl has already kicked you. She preferred a software engineer to an MA in Hindi. It's time you focused on your career. Wasting your time will get you nowhere.'

'Let's eat. We are getting late,' said Manoj gently.

Pandey hadn't reacted to Avinash's taunts, though he was smouldering with resentment. He didn't dare say anything to Yogita. But now he ran out of patience and Manoj found himself on the receiving end of his anger. 'I'll see how much you enjoy your meal the day Shraddha leaves you. What do you care? You must be missing Shraddha. Go and call her up. You don't have to worry about me.'

Manoj sensed that reacting to Pandey at this stage might backfire, so he kept quiet. Avinash had to drag Pandey away from him. The DJ meanwhile, was belting out the song *'Kambakht ishq hai jo, sara jahan hai wo'*. Some people were dancing to its beat. Sukhvinder Singh and Asha Bhosle's song drifted into Manoj's mind afar, to his own incomplete love story. He felt as if the song was being played for him. The music conjured up pleasant memories of Shraddha.

So, one lover's heart felt light, whereas another's heavy. Pandey found himself in a dilemma—to eat or not to eat. There was a brief but vigorous tussle between his heart and stomach. He was not going to get any dinner even in Peelikothi today. He decided not to compromise on food. And having eaten to their fill, the three of them left in the car. The food gave Pandey fresh energy to express his sorrows. He stared at the road and wanted to cry. But the car didn't appear to him a suitable place to burst into tears.

While driving, Avinash delivered another sermon. 'Take my word for it, girls are like sweet poison for those who are preparing for any competitive exam. If you don't keep your distance, they will ruin you for sure.' His words of wisdom had no effect on the duo. However, he continued with unabated enthusiasm. 'Lovers are dogs running after girls all the time, willing to lap up whatever is thrown at them without worrying about their studies. Isn't it true, Pandey?'

Avinash had called Pandey a dog and wanted him to accept it.

'Yes, I am a dog; a dog, indeed,' shouted Pandey in a frenzy and broke down, clasping Avinash in his arms. Somehow Avinash pushed him away and said, 'Let me drive carefully or I may ram the car into someone. You have just lost your love; you may well lose your life.'

Manoj was singing cheerfully to himself. Avinash asked him, 'Have I said anything wrong?'

In response, Manoj sang the lyrics of the hit they had just left behind, at the top of his voice: *'Ye ishq, ishq himmat hai, ye ishq, ishq kismet hai, ye ishq, ishq tagat hai, ye ishq dil ki daulat hai'*. The song was so loud and out of tune that they caught the attention of passers-by.

On reaching Peelikothi, they realized that it was hard to go back to studying that night. Lying listlessly in his room, Pandey lamented over the loss of his love. Instead of listening to a romantic song, today he played a bhajan from the film *Lagaan*— *'O Palanhare, nirgun aur nyare, tum bin hamra kounu nahin, hamri uljhan suljhao bhagwan, tum bin hamra kounu nahin'*. He immersed himself in the bhakti of God, imploring Him to show the right path, and then proceeded to shed tears in bed. With Manoj lost in thoughts of Shraddha, the lovers had once again become oblivious to the threat of the approaching prelims exam.

33

The result of prelims had come out. This was Manoj's second attempt and Pandey's first. Neither of them got through it. For Manoj, it was like playing the game of snakes and ladders— he had put one foot forward wrong and he was now back at the start. But Avinash and Naval had done exceptionally well. Having steered through the first stage of the battle with flying colours, Naval was itching to humiliate his enemies. With a grin of triumph on his face, he shot his first arrow: 'Pandey, Aishwarya Rai has ruined your career.'

Pandey was in no mood to listen to jokes or deal with riddles. Annoyed, he asked, 'Which Aishwarya Rai?'

'The girl with the big dark eyes who left you. And because of whom you couldn't prepare for the exam thoroughly,' scoffed Naval.

'You've got it all wrong,' said Pandey defending himself. 'It's not about any girl. In this year's history paper, they unexpectedly asked more questions from the prehistoric cultures in India and south Indian kingdoms. We hadn't gone through these topics well.'

'We have to cover the entire syllabus properly. If one reads selectively, one is bound to invite disaster and fail in the exam,' said Avinash bluntly.

Manoj was the duo's next target. 'You got through the prelims once, but failed your second attempt,' Naval said. 'It's a matter of grave concern.' Before Manoj could respond, he turned to

Avinash and said, 'I don't see any point in staying here now. Let's leave tomorrow for Delhi and get ourselves enrolled in a good coaching centre.' He stood up and, humming the song '*Naach na jaane angan tedha*' from the film *Padosan* while looking at Pandey, slowly left the room. Like its singer Manna Dey, Naval made sure to sing the word 'tedha' in different ways before walking into his room. Pandey and Manoj felt completely helpless at these taunts, but kept quiet.

Manoj's confidence was badly dented. He knew by now that each time he failed he would have to start from scratch. A success in a previous attempt was no guarantee of success in the next. When one flunked the prelims, how could one even imagine getting through the mains and the interview? His success in the first attempt had become meaningless now. The reality of the fiercely competitive exams became clear to him.

'No wonder it's so tough to get through these exams,' he thought. There were zillions who dreamt big, but fortune smiled on only a few. To get a headstart on thousands and lakhs of competitors, one had to toil day and night. Naval and Avinash were his neighbours. If he couldn't outshine them, how could he stand out from the rest who were even more diligent—competitors from all over the country, who were ready to put their heart and soul into the preparation of the exam.

The only ray of hope he still had was Vikas Sir's compliments on his answers in Hindi literature. His evaluation of that one answer script gave Manoj fresh energy. Despite meeting many failures, the idea of quitting never crossed his mind. The only option that he had was to exercise patience and to keep trying. The UP state PSC mains was his next target, but its dates were yet to be announced; the all-India UPSC prelims would be held in May next year. He had to be mentally prepared for the long haul.

However, despite his recent failure, he was unable to forget Shraddha even for a moment. For two months, he studied with ruthless determination only for his heart to ache as her memories would come flooding back. Her dazzling face, radiant smile and velvety voice wouldn't let him sleep. It's not easy to bear the pain of love and separation. He was overwhelmed by a longing for the time spent with her. His days began with her thoughts, and nights ended with her in his dreams.

One evening, as he stood on the terrace gloomily watching the sun sink below the horizon, Pandey read him a brief sermon: 'Love has undone both of us, Manoj,' he said. 'Now we should put everything aside and immerse ourselves in books.' Ever since Yogita had left him for a more suitable boy, Pandey had started preaching about the side effects of love.

'I couldn't pass the exam because of my wrong strategy,' replied Manoj, his eyes fixed on the setting sun. 'My love for Shraddha inspires me to work harder.'

Unlike Pandey, he didn't hold his beloved responsible for his failure. Rather, he gave her the credit for bolstering his confidence. 'What Shraddha means to me, you can never understand,' he told Pandey. 'She occupies all my waking thoughts. When I sleep, I dream of her. You may call it love, but for me it's a bhakti that gives me strength.'

Love, devotion, fear, faith, dedication and a hundred other sentiments were combined into one. Pandey finally stopped convincing him to change his mind and instead proposed, 'Let's go and meet Tyagiji. He is a great motivator.' They hadn't met him for a long time. They went over to his house and found him reclining on the bed, engrossed in a book. He greeted his visitors with a broad smile and asked, 'How are your studies going on?'

Manoj was about to reply, but Pandey interrupted, 'No more studies, only bhakti.'

'Bhakti for whom?' asked Tyagiji baffled.

'Shraddha's bhakti,' replied Pandey, his eyes glinting with mischief. Manoj felt as though bomb had exploded. He couldn't believe that someone could talk so indiscreetly before a school principal who was a disciplinarian like Tyagiji. Perhaps, Pandey had planned all along to expose him. Having revealed his friend's secret, Pandey was waiting for Tyagiji's reaction. Manoj, on the other hand, was flushed with embarrassment. He wanted to run away, but couldn't move an inch.

Before the school principal could even ask anything further, Pandey started with the story. 'Manoj was in love with Shraddha until a few days ago, and now he realizes that it's not love but bhakti. You know everything. I'm sure you too have some colourful stories of your own. Since you are pretty experienced, we want to listen to you on this very touching subject.'

Having exposed Manoj, Pandey was now itching to learn about any love story hiding in Tyagiji's younger days.

'Ha ha. Not so colourful,' replied Tyagiji, laughing heartily. The laughter and open response took Manoj by surprise.

'Would you mind telling us the name of the person you were in love with?' asked Pandey, rubbing his hands.

'She must have grown old now,' replied the principal, still in good humour.

Manoj could only gape at the two of them in astonishment.

Thankfully, Pandey bestowed a favour on Tyagiji by not pushing him to reveal the name of his old love; instead, he went back to describing his friend's frame of mind. 'Manojji can't live without talking to Shraddha. His mind is distracted, though he insists that she boosts his confidence and inspires him to study.'

'If there is love,' responded Tyagiji, 'the question of distraction does not arise. Love makes one pure-hearted, puts one at ease, sweeps away negative thoughts, and enhances the powers of concentration. When one is in love, one does everything with renewed enthusiasm, pure joy, and single-minded determination.' Tyagiji's views on love appealed to Manoj.

'But there is a catch,' said Pandey, determined to added spice to the situation. 'Shraddha doesn't love him.'

'Let her not love him,' said Tyagiji, 'that is the beauty of love. It doesn't require the other person to love you back. Manoj loves Shraddha. It doesn't affect her. It is Manoj who is getting enriched. It is Manoj who is becoming pure-hearted by the experience. As the poet says, "Your love makes me admire the entire universe." Because of his love for Shraddha, one day Manoj will be able to love all the creatures of the world. It's truly a rewarding experience.'

Tyagiji had showed them a novel side of love. His soothing words gave Manoj the courage to share his thoughts. 'I agree entirely with what you have said. But why do I feel tense? Why do I get distracted?'

Tyagiji replied with a gentle smile, 'There is no place for expectations and desires in pure love. It's within your rights to love someone. The rest doesn't matter. Your problem is that you want Shraddha to love you back. If your love is shackled by desire, it's bound to fade away. You can control your mind, but not someone else's.'

Pandey used this opportunity to share his pain with Tyagiji. 'I think it's not possible to get someone's love without being successful.'

'What's the relation between love and success?' Tyagiji asked. 'If you are successful, you will get love; if you aren't, love will be beyond your reach. What kind of theory is this, bhai? And what is success? To become a tehsildar or a thanedar? Just as people don't get what love is, they fail to understand what success is.

Is success acquiring power, prestige, and money? I am of the opinion that if one does any work with the utmost sincerity and happiness, one is successful in every sense of the word. Then it's of little importance whether you become a thanedar or sweep the streets in the morning.'

Pandey had been quite hopeful that Tyagiji would deter Manoj from getting carried away and advise him to take his studies seriously, but all his expectations were turned upside down. Manoj, on the other hand, believed each and every word the old man had said. Manoj and Pandey returned to Peelikothi—one satisfied, the other dissatisfied.

Tyagiji had advised Manoj to keep his feelings to himself, to give precedence to experience over expression. He realized there was no need to talk about his love for Shraddha. If he showed courage and moral strength, someday she would definitely fall in love with him. For the next few days, he didn't call Shraddha. But for how long could he manage without expressing what lay in his heart?

Doubts started tormenting him—one moment, he felt an abiding love for her, the next moment his sentiments would waver. How short-lived human emotions are; a moment of absolute trust is followed by moments of deep distrust. Then would come a flood of love, longing and her memories, which would sweep away all doubt; but for love all else appeared transitory. Love is indeed strange.

After exercising self-control for a few days, Manoj thought to himself, 'I won't say a word about love, but at least I'll get to hear her silky voice. That should be enough to put me at ease for another two to three months. What if Shraddha has forgotten me? If she hasn't, does she remember me as much as I do? I must know how she has been and for that I'll have to call her up.'

He plucked up enough courage to dial her number. Since he had made up his mind not to broach the subject of love, the conversation revolved around books and careers. Shraddha told him that she had completed her internship and was leaving for Delhi to resume her preparation. This was encouraging news. Manoj too got ready to set off for Delhi, to prepare for his third attempt and to enjoy Shraddha's company.

34

Delhi. Mukherjee Nagar. Manoj was waiting for Shraddha at the park across the road from Drishti Coaching Centre. Two days ago, he and Pandey had rented a room at Nehru Vihar, and resumed their studies. Manoj's father luckily hadn't been suspended yet. At present, he was posted in Jhabua, so the finances of the house were stable. Mother had given him Rs 5,000 this time when he left home. Avinash and Naval had already come to Delhi, rented a room in Gandhi Vihar, and taken the main exam. Following his friends, Gupta too arrived in the national capital and stayed right next to Avinash in Gandhi Vihar.

Shraddha had shifted into the same hostel in Mukherjee Nagar, where she had stayed earlier. It was Manoj's lucky day as he was going to meet her. When he spotted her from a distance in a bright-red salwar-kameez printed with black flowers, his anxieties were put to rest. She appeared like a shower of rain in a parched desert, or welcome shade for a wayfarer in the scorching heat. Was this going to be a fresh start or would his hopes be shattered again, Manoj wondered.

There was a moment's silence before Shraddha asked, 'How is life?'

'Everything is fine. I am back. Let us see what the city has in store for me,' Manoj said, his voice calm.

'The city will make you work hard. We should give our 100 per cent,' said Shraddha. 'Success will definitely come our way.'

Her company mattered the most and what could be a better way of spending time together than studying with her. When he proposed this to Shraddha, she readily agreed.

From the next day, they began studying Hindi literature for two hours daily in Manoj's room, after which he would walk her back. One day, on their way back, Manoj said, 'If we do the kind of intensive reading that we have done in the last one month for at least a year, we shall definitely get through the exam.'

'We won't stop until we succeed,' she added.

Shraddha was determined to achieve her goal. In her company, Manoj too was quite hopeful that if they slogged it out as a team, success would be within their reach. They reached the hostel and she stood for a while, and then said, 'I need to go to Batra to buy a book rack. Would you like to come along?' This was what Manoj secretly wished for, to be with her as long as possible.

Shraddha bought a rack and would have called a rickshaw, but Manoj intervened: 'It's very light. I can easily carry it.' Without waiting for her response, he placed it on his shoulder and walked on with a cheerful smile. When they reached the hostel, she thanked him, her face lit up with affection. After chatting for a few minutes, he sought her permission to leave. She nodded with a smile and watched him until he was out of sight.

Manoj found Pandey quite upset when he entered the room. 'Why are you so late?' Pandey asked curtly.

'I was helping Shraddha buy a rack.'

As long as Pandey remained in love with Yogita, he supported Manoj—so much so that he had inspired him to travel all the way to Almora. But the moment Yogita chose someone else, he had changed colours like a chameleon. Now he warned Manoj, 'Shraddha is very clever. She doesn't love you. She comes here only to seek help in Hindi literature. These girls are shrewd enough to know how to get their work done. Today she made you carry her book rack, tomorrow she may ask you to do something else. At Mukherjee Nagar, girls befriend boys so that they get someone to do their work for free. Take my word for it, Shraddha is no different.'

Manoj didn't appreciate these remarks. However, he ignored them, still overwhelmed by the affectionate glance that Shraddha had cast at him today.

35

The Delhi Book Fair was on at Pragati Maidan. When Shraddha asked Manoj to accompany her, he wholeheartedly agreed. She bought a few books, while Manoj flipped through some before placing them back on the table. The biographies of Vivekanand, Bhagat Singh, and Lincoln especially drew his attention.

'Do you want to buy them? The memoirs of these eminent persons are truly inspiring,' said Shraddha.

'I've already gone through all of them. Lincoln's life story fascinated me so much that I read it at least four times,' he replied. He was pleased to display his erudition before the one whose opinion mattered the most to him.

'When did you read all of them?' she asked, pleasantly surprised.

This gave him one more chance to create a good impression on her. 'I had finished them all during my BA,' he said enthusiastically.

'Have you really read so much?' Shraddha asked, her eyes wide with surprise.

'Yes, I used to work at a library in Gwalior. Back then, I read as much as I could.'

As they were talking, he picked up APJ Abdul Kalam's autobiography, *Wings of Fire* but as soon as he saw its price, he put it back and walked out of the stall. They both went to a coffee shop, where Shraddha plonked her books on a table and slumped into a chair. Having explored so many stalls in the last three hours, she was exhausted. Manoj got a coffee for her and she thanked him with a smile.

For quite some time now, he had been itching to share his innermost feelings with her. Gathering courage from the air of festivity at the book fair, he said, 'Shraddha, I have something to say.' The change of expression on his face betrayed his thoughts. 'You should pay attention to English essay as well as grammar. I suggest that you devote one hour daily to English,' replied Shraddha, steering the conversation away to studies. But Manoj's mind was in turmoil.

'Aren't you listening?' she asked, as if trying to wake him up from deep sleep.

'Shraddha, who should I listen to? You or your eyes? You say something and your eyes say something else.'

She fixed her gaze on the cup of coffee before her and said, 'I can teach you how to write an essay in simple English. You can't afford to repeat the mistake that you committed in your first attempt.' Under the pretext of teaching him English, Shraddha had thrown cold water on his plans. He had resolved to talk about his feelings, but now he fumbled for the right words. Having finished her coffee, she said, 'I forgot a book of mine at the stall. I'll be back in a moment.'

Five minutes later, she strode up to the table with the book and said, 'This is for you.'

Wings of Fire, the book Manoj couldn't afford, was lying in his hands now. He turned the first page and found 'For Manoj's wings' penned down on it.

'Did you know that I wanted to buy this book?' he asked Shraddha. Without uttering a word, she picked up all her books from the table, her eyes fixed on his face.

While looking at the cover page, Manoj said, 'You are a remarkably good reader.'

'How?' asked a surprised Shraddha.

'Because you can read my mind.' He hadn't given up trying to convey what he had felt for so long. But Shraddha was also adamant about not walking down the path that he wanted her to. 'Let's go, we are getting late,' she said, avoiding what he had actually said, and they both walked to the bus stop. Later, sitting next to Manoj in the bus, Shraddha stared out of the window and wondered how one could experience so much peace and happiness by just giving such a small gift to someone.

Manoj returned to his room elated that evening and showed the book to Pandey, who was sulking in bed, pained that his friend had taken a stroll at the book fair with a girl, while he lay listless and alone in his room. Pandey flipped open the book, turned to the title page and read aloud—'For Manoj's wings'.

'Oh, I see. Now you are to be motivated by this book gifted by your girlfriend and not by the poverty of your family? One gets through an exam by reading the books of the syllabus, Manojji. These useless books will do you no good,' scoffed Pandey and flung the book on the bed. Manoj was enraged, but with great self-restraint, he managed to reply calmly, 'It's always good to read motivational books. You never know when that information will come in handy.'

This annoyed Pandey further. 'When you are in love, everything that your beloved says sounds motivational,' he snapped. 'I had high hopes of you. Your struggle and seriousness towards the goal made me feel that you would certainly become successful one day. Unfortunately, you have entangled yourself in love and things are going downhill. It's for your own good that I am advising you to stay away from Shraddha. Otherwise, this one-sided love will get you nowhere.'

Manoj explained his philosophy of love once more to Pandey. 'You know it well how important Shraddha is to me. Nothing is hidden from you. It's because of her that I take my studies even more seriously. Her presence helps me in every possible way—'

'That's utter rubbish,' retorted Pandey, 'It's necessary to exercise control over your emotions and actions.'

Manoj could take no more of Pandey's hypocrisy, and burst out, 'As long as you had Yogita in your life, you had no problem with Shraddha. And now that she is gone, Shraddha has become a thorn in your side.'

'How dare you!' said Pandey trembling with rage, and springing to his feet. 'You have to decide right away whether you want to live with Shraddha or me. If she sets her foot in this room, I can no longer remain your roommate. Choose between her and me.'

Manoj had never envisioned matters would come this; that Pandey would be so adamant. Miserably, he answered, 'I can't live without Shraddha.'

'This is what I had expected of you,' said Pandey, and packed his books and clothes. Peeling the paper off the wall where he had penned down all the fundamental rights from the Constitution of India, he said, 'You may well paste your girlfriend's photo here. Why do you need to mug up the fundamental rights now? Staring at her picture will be enough to pass the exam.' And before Manoj could respond to his taunt, a furious Pandey stomped out of the room.

36

One day, Avinash and Naval came running to Manoj's room and said anxiously, 'Cops have arrested Gupta. He has been taken to the Mukherjee Nagar Police Station. We better hurry.'

The three of them barged into the police station and found Gupta perched on a stool, frightened. A constable was rebuking him, 'If I file a case against you, your career will be destroyed. You won't get even a peon's job. Forget about the IAS then. Tell me, should I file the case?'

Manoj, equally frightened by the cop's behaviour, managed a courteous enquiry, 'What happened, sir? What has he done?'

As soon as the constable noticed that three friends of an accused had burst into the police station, he got even more annoyed and said, 'Bhaisahib was drinking alcohol behind the Batra cinema hall. When I forbade him to drink, he boasted that he was a DSP posted in Madhya Pradesh and was preparing for civil services in Delhi. He even warned me to stay within my limits. I asked him where was he posted in MP, but he fumbled. I come across such fake cops daily. A case will be lodged against him for drinking in a public place.'

Gupta had landed himself in hot water because of his lies and addiction to alcohol, his friends realized. Avinash leaned over and whispered in the constable's ear, 'Forgive him this once, sir. Overburdened with studies, he has lapsed into depression. He won't commit such a blunder again.'

To pacify the cop, Naval slapped Gupta on the head. 'You liar! You should be ashamed of yourself. How dare you misbehave with sir! You owe him an apology.' At this, Gupta flung himself at the cop's feet.

'Sir, please give him a chance to mend his ways,' begged Manoj.

The constable's anger subsided as quickly as it had flared up. He was accustomed to such cases in Mukherjee Nagar, and normally let such miscreants off with a warning and mild threats. Gupta was also released with a solemn warning. 'Your parents have pinned all their hopes on your getting a job. So focus on your studies and don't fool around.'

To Manoj, the cop came across as a kind-hearted person. He thanked the policeman profusely and they all returned to Gandhi Vihar. But Gupta was seething with resentment. 'I won't spare that constable,' he burst out. 'The only aim of my life from now on is to become an IPS officer and suspend him.' No one paid any attention to his babbling.

After vacating Manoj's room some five days ago, Pandey had moved in with Gupta. His anger against Manoj hadn't abated yet. So when he saw Manoj enter, he looked the other way.

37

Manoj had made up his mind to ask his father to send him Rs 2,000 per month for a year, so that he could focus on his studies. He called him from a telephone booth, but before he could spell out his problem, the father exploded, 'Scoundrels! I tell you all of them are bastards. No one is bothered about the country. The fool suspended me again. I won't remain silent and will bring the deputy director to his senses. I've thrown down a challenge that I may starve but won't backtrack.'

It was hard for Manoj to figure out the reason behind his father's suspension, but it became pretty clear that he should expect no financial support from home. He returned to his room disappointed, and concluded that the only valuable lesson he could take from his father was his tenacity and his never-say-die spirit. While he was mulling over his father's nature and his future course of action, Shraddha entered the room.

'Will you walk with me to the Hanuman Temple in Nehru Vihar?' Manoj asked her.

They both walked to the temple, where Manoj sat down and closed his eyes before the statue of Lord Hanuman. After his contemplation, he went to Shraddha and shared, 'Today, I've taken a pledge that no matter how adverse the circumstances are, I won't flinch from the course of duty. Whether I get success or not, I'll work with honesty and integrity, and follow my father's principles.'

The eagerly awaited response was supportive, 'I don't see any reason why you shouldn't succeed!' With her approval, his zeal for success grew manifold. He stepped outside, his mind imbued with self-respect and confidence. As they walked out of the temple, they saw some people were begging and asking for help. These people, Manoj found out, were not beggars but farm labourers from Bundelkhand. Even after running from pillar to post in Delhi for several days, they hadn't been able to land a job. Since they had run out of money, there was no other option but to beg for money to pay their return fare. 'How much money do you need to return to your village?' Manoj asked.

'A thousand rupees,' the eldest answered.

Without wasting even a fraction of a second, Manoj pulled out a Rs 100 from his pocket and handed it to the man. 'You don't need to worry. You'll get one thousand rupees,' he reassured him. As they walked back, Shraddha chided him. 'What have you done? This was the only note that you had. God knows if they are telling the truth. This could be a ploy to make money.'

'It's quite possible he was telling a lie,' agreed Manoj, 'but the issue is not whether these people are right or wrong. What matters is how I, as an individual, respond to someone's misery. I can see they are needy, and all that I care about is how to help them. All suspicions are groundless before my resolve to help them reach home.'

Puzzled, Shraddha asked him, 'Do you have that much money?'

'No,' said Manoj.

'How will you manage then?' she said, completely flummoxed.

'No matter what,' replied Manoj, 'I've decided to give them one thousand.' Overwhelmed by their plight, his mind had ceased to be guided by the logic and reason of this cut-throat world. Setting aside his hesitation in approaching strangers, he spoke to everyone nearby, including the shopkeepers, about the labourers' problems and asked for money. Some ignored his request, others thought he was insane. Neither the passers-by nor the shopkeepers gave him any money. Unable to dissuade him from begging, Shraddha followed him quietly.

Manoj was adamant on collecting the money. He went to the temple again and narrated the entire story to the priest. 'Son, all kinds of people come here and ask for money. How can I help everyone?' he replied.

'There is no one as pure-hearted and generous as you.' Manoj tried to persuade him. 'My heart is flooded with deep respect the moment I look at you. You are close to God and know his leela better than mere mortals like us. We never know when God may turn up before us in the form of a human. That little child over there! She looks at you with a lot of hope! You know it well that Swami Vivekanand had said, "If you want to find God, serve man."'

Manoj paused for his response. The priest's heart was beginning to melt; he turned his eyes to the poor man's family. This is what Manoj had hoped for. Since he didn't want to miss this opportunity, he suggested, 'If you request the devotees to help these people, they will surely listen to you.' The priest had been serving the temple for the last thirty years. No one had praised him so profusely until today. He felt inclined to offer a helping hand to the labourers and said, 'I agree with you, beta. Let's do something.'

For the next one hour, the priest appealed for donations and most of the devotees obliged him. Soon a sum of Rs 900 was collected. Having thanked the priest heartily, Manoj gave the entire amount to the labourers. That day, Shraddha saw a different side of Manoj. She wanted to speak to him, but couldn't utter a word. They walked to Nehru Vihar in complete silence, Shraddha's heart filled with pure joy at the miracle Manoj had pulled off.

38

It was a crucial phase of his life as both the UP PCS mains and the UPSC prelims were round the corner. And it was also at this juncture that Manoj realized that he was not going to get any financial support from his family. Without it, he couldn't have prolonged his stay in an expensive city like Delhi. When Pandey had stayed with him, he had somehow managed the rent, but now that he was gone, Manoj needed a roommate. Otherwise, he would have to pay the Rs 1500 rent by himself.

He was also a part of a group of three students who had together hired a cook to prepare their meals in the shared kitchen. The other two members of this group included a senior student named Varun living in the next room and his roommate. This arrangement was overall useful and pocket-friendly. But now that Manoj had run out of money, how could he continue to be a part of this group! The thought troubled him.

'Varun Sir, why don't we fire the cook?' Manoj suggested to his senior. 'These days he prepares tasteless food. Besides, he is always late. I can cook on his behalf. I'll also buy the vegetables and groceries from the market. In exchange for work, I won't pay for my food because my father is not in a situation to support me.' Varun and his roommate were already sick and tired of their lazy cook. They liked Manoj's offer. Other than cooking, he would also have to do some menial jobs, such as washing the dishes and mopping the floors.

Then, one day, a student called Sharad came to Delhi from Gwalior to prepare for the competitive exams and he became Manoj's new roomie. Now, even though the issues of food and rent were solved, Manoj's problems were far from over. He shared them with Shraddha. 'I'll have to do some odd jobs to stay afloat in the city. My food has been taken care of. I've started cooking for my friends. Even then, I'll need at least one thousand rupees for rent plus other expenses.'

'Let's go to Vikas Sir,' she suggested. 'You may land a job in his coaching centre.'

'No, I can't discuss my problems with him. He has high hopes of my success. I don't want to disappoint him.' Manoj's self-respect wouldn't let him beg for help from Sir.

'It's alright,' said Shraddha. 'Let's go to some other coaching, then. You'll get a job somewhere for sure,' she consoled him.

They went to several institutes in Mukherjee Nagar, but to no avail. Someone offered Manoj an eight-hour job to counsel students who flocked to the centre seeking information. At another coaching centre, they needed a mains-qualified candidate to prepare study materials. Manoj found himself undergoing the same nerve-wracking experience that he had gone through while looking for a job in Gwalior.

He walked Shraddha to her hostel gate and trod heavily towards Nehru Vihar.

At some distance from her hostel, right outside a bungalow, he saw eight to ten cars parked and a young boy washing them. Manoj asked him, 'Bhaiya, how much do you get for this job?'

'Why should I tell you?' the boy shot back.

Manoj hadn't expected such a curt response. However, he gathered his courage and rang the doorbell of the bungalow. Dogs could be heard barking furiously from within. Frightened, he took two steps back. When a lady finally stepped out, Manoj asked, 'Ma'am, I can wash cars. May I get a job here?'

The lady seemed to be quite gentle and well mannered. She replied, 'No, bhaiya. Our driver usually cleans the car. Today, he is on leave so I sent for this boy.' Dismayed, Manoj turned to leave. As he was making his way back to his room, the boy washing cars suddenly called out and said that the lady wanted to meet him.

He hurried back to the gate and found her waiting. 'Can you take out our dogs for a walk in the evening for two hours daily?' she asked.

The proposal threw Manoj off balance for a moment. He had never imagined or heard of anyone making money by walking other people's dogs. He was also apprehensive whether others would approve of this sort of job. 'You'll get eight hundred rupees per month,' the woman said.

Perhaps the woman was in dire need of part-time help. No wonder she was offering such a handsome amount of money for a two-hour-a-day job. But would this suit him? Wouldn't his friends make fun of him? Then he thought to himself, 'Just as others teach, work in a coaching centre, wash cars, pull a rickshaw, and do all kinds of odd jobs in order to make a living, I can take out dogs for a stroll. If one does one's work with sincerity and honesty, there is no shame and no harm in it.'

The lady gave him Rs 500 in advance and Manoj was quite relieved that he could now stay afloat in Delhi. Shraddha was the first one with whom he wanted to share this news. 'She'll be delighted,' he said to himself. Elated, he rushed to her hostel and was about to ring the doorbell when it suddenly crossed his mind how would she react to his walking dogs to earn a living. Could a girl ever accept a dog walker as a lover? His enthusiasm dampened, he returned to his room without meeting her.

Thereafter, every evening, Manoj walked Shraddha to her room and discreetly left to do his new job. Scared of bumping into any of her or his friends while on the job, he decided to walk the dogs around the drain behind the narrow Nehru Vihar Bridge, which was usually not crowded. But one day, his worst fears came true. Around 10 p.m., on his way back to return the dogs, he ran into Shraddha. Astounded, she asked, 'Whose doggies are these?'

Manoj didn't know what to say, but finally told her the truth about his eight-hundred-rupee job and waited for her reaction. Stunned by his story, she felt a tide rising in her heart and controlled her emotions, lest tears should brim over and flow down her cheeks. 'I have a request,' she finally said, her voice calm.

Manoj, afraid that Shraddha might ask him to quit this menial job, hesitated a moment and said, 'Tell me.'

'Can I come with you from tomorrow?'

'Won't you feel uncomfortable walking someone else's dogs with me?' Manoj asked. She shook her head.

One evening, Manoj and Shraddha went to Gandhi Vihar to meet Pandey. On reaching there, they were startled to see an IPS officer in his room. It took them a while to figure out that it was Gupta who was wearing the police uniform. Pandey was not in the room. Sitting on a chair, Gupta was reading a book. On his shoulders were epaulettes, adorned with a stainless steel 'IPS' and stars.

'What's this?' asked Manoj, baffled.

Brimming with confidence, Gupta shared his secret strategy with them. 'Look at the badge and the stars, Manoj. They motivate me to work hard and become an IPS officer. These days, I wear this uniform while studying. It strengthens my resolve to become a police officer and suspend that constable. I won't spare him, no matter what.' Gupta had not forgotten the humiliation; he had been working on a comprehensive strategy to exact revenge on the poor cop.

It was evident that the incident had left an indelible mark on Gupta. But Shraddha was fascinated by the police uniform. On their way back, she said, 'You'll look incredibly handsome in the IPS uniform.'

Manoj replied in jest, 'Okay, Shraddha. I'll ask Gupta where he bought it from. I'll also wear it from tomorrow and then sit down to study.'

She burst out laughing and said, 'No, I want you to join the IPS.'

'As you command, boss,' Manoj responded light-heartedly. A radiant smile spread across her face. As they were strolling along, Manoj noticed Pandey at a distance and walked up to meet him. But Pandey turned his eyes away and hurried past them.

39

The result of UP PCS mains, held some two months ago, was out. No one from the Gwalior group got through, except Avinash. Manoj was terribly upset about his failure even though he had left several answers incomplete. The question on the history of race riots in Britain had stumped him. He was also unhappy with his answers on the Chartist movement, the American Civil War, and democracy in ancient India. His preparation was far from thorough. Dejected, he slumped into a chair, with no other choice but to assess his failure.

Shraddha understood his state of mind and encouraged him, saying, 'You shouldn't be disheartened. It won't do you any good. You should reflect on your mistakes and learn from them. This will help you eventually climb the ladder of success. I think you should get coaching for general studies and history. Without it, you may not get good marks in these papers.'

'You are absolutely right.' He too had figured out that he couldn't do well in the PSC exam because of lack of proper guidance.

He returned to his village to arrange money for the coaching classes. His father hadn't come home for several months. When he told his mother about the problem, she began to curse the father. 'From where shall I arrange money? Your useless father has sworn an oath that he won't do his job well. He doesn't care even if his children beg for food in the streets.'

'Everything will be alright. Once I get a job, you won't face any problem,' Manoj reassured her. Though far from success, he showed his mother a ray of hope. 'I've no money right now,' she replied, 'but I am planning to keep a buffalo. Our neighbour Rakesh has one. He has agreed to lend it to me. I'll sell its milk and take care of the household expenses.'

Manoj held back his tears at the hardships his aging mother was having to endure. The condition of his impoverished family was so glaringly different from the affluent world of Delhi. He wondered whether he would ever be able to do anything to change the fortunes of his family. For the next four days, he tried all possible means, but failed to arrange the money. When his mother saw his glum face, she quietly borrowed some money and gave it to him.

Back in Delhi, Shraddha had begun to feel terribly lonely, though Manoj had left just five days ago. She tried to catch up with her female friends, whom she hadn't met for several days, despite living in the same hostel as them. Within a few minutes, their conversations bored her to death. Though she was used to staying alone in the hostel, she had never felt so empty. On her way to and from the coaching centre, her eyes scanned the crowd desperately looking for that one face, but he was not to be seen. Her ears longed to listen to a voice that could not be heard. Time and again, she looked at the road her balcony overlooked, but her eyes couldn't spot the man she pined for.

How far was Manoj's village? Where did he live exactly? She had no idea. Nor did she have the phone number of his house. She felt like going to Gandhi Vihar to meet his friends; Pandey might have his number or that of one of his neighbours. But she couldn't gather the courage to approach them. Finally, left with no option, she tried to immerse herself in a book, but found it hard to concentrate for even half an hour. Her tiffin remained unfinished as if she had lost her appetite. She felt strange.

When Manoj was around, she had made it clear to him that they should study together as friends; he shouldn't have any other expectation of her. God knows what spell he had cast on her that she felt restless in his absence. Her situation today was similar to that of Manoj's, when he had travelled all the way to Almora just to meet her. She empathized with him now, but could do nothing except waiting for him.

The day Manoj returned to Delhi, he went straight to Shraddha's hostel and rang her doorbell. She came down instantly as if she had grown a pair of wings. Her heart leapt with joy as her loneliness ended in a flash. By the time they reached his room, her eyes were brimming with tears. She sat on a chair and closed her eyes. For how long could she fight back the tears—one or two rolled down her cheek slowly. Silence fell over the room for the next five minutes. Then, she drew a long breath, a sigh of relief. All the pain, loneliness and sorrow of the last five days vanished.

'What happened?' asked Manoj. Perhaps now he could read her mind. Shraddha was unable to speak. Fixing her unblinking gaze on him, she tried to smile lest her tears betray her thoughts. A tearful smile spread across her face. Her eyes expressed love, her smile tried to conceal it. Shraddha wanted to share her thoughts with Manoj, but couldn't. He waited with bated breath to listen to her. In his absence, she had grown restless for a glimpse of him. Her turbulent mind calmed as soon as he turned up and all her anxieties were allayed.

It took her a while to compose herself. A gentle smile lit up her face. She got up from the chair, picked up the monthly *Pratiyogita Darpan*, gave it to Manoj and said, 'You have already wasted quite a few days at home. Now you better return to your studies. There is a well-written essay in the magazine on India's achievements in the space sector. Read it aloud.'

'It's impossible to win over this girl,' Manoj thought, and started reading the essay half-heartedly, 'The sky and the stars glimmering across it have stood as the source of mystery and attraction for human beings since antiquity.'

40

Manoj was keen to take coaching for the history and general studies papers. The money that he had brought from home took care of history, but there was none left for the other. Shraddha and he had both qualified in the prelims, meanwhile. It was his third attempt and Shraddha's first. Avinash and Naval too had got through. They hadn't succeeded in the last mains exam. Once again, they got a chance to write the mains. Gupta, on the other hand, couldn't qualify. Pandey, even after parting ways with Manoj, had failed. He was still unable to discover a foolproof plan to get through the exam. Manoj had qualified despite being in love; Pandey, who kept himself away from girls and considered them a complete waste of time, hadn't.

Failure in the last UPSC mains had worn down Naval's enthusiasm, but now he was again in high spirits. Emboldened by his success, he felt tempted to make fun of Pandey and taunted, 'The one who is in love passed the exam and you failed. What do you have to say, Pandey?'

Since Pandey had really worked hard after shifting to Gupta's room, he was baffled; he couldn't figure out what had gone wrong. His own failure coupled with Manoj's success left him resentful and jealous. 'He has only passed the prelims,' he said to Naval. 'There is still a long way to go. If you are in love, you can't get through such a tough exam. I'm making a prediction: he won't qualify in the mains, let alone get selected in the final list.'

Meanwhile, Shraddha continued to come to Manoj's room daily to study. They chatted during their breaks. It seemed impossible to cover such a vast syllabus. What to study! How to study! For history and Hindi, Manoj read notes that he had brought from the coaching centre. His progress in general studies was not satisfactory and he still worked as a dog walker for two hours daily to sustain himself.

Manoj, Shraddha, Avinash, and Naval appeared for the mains, and eagerly waited for the results. Manoj was not happy with his answers in the general studies paper. In history and Hindi literature too his answers were not succinct. For some reason, he couldn't recall all the points in the exam. While writing about fundamental duties, he mentioned only six—the rest he forgot. His answer on the features of the Devanagari script was also a bit of a let-down. Overall, he hadn't performed well in the exams, and Shraddha's situation was no different.

The results were declared. As expected, Manoj and Shraddha didn't clear the mains. Manoj had wasted three of his four attempts by now; he hadn't been able to pass the mains even once. Naval's result was equally dismal. But Avinash had done wonders; his name figured in the final list of the selected candidates and he became a deputy collector in DANICS—Delhi, Andaman, and Nicobar Islands Civil Service. However, he continued his preparation for the next attempt, hoping to become an IAS officer. Some days later, the UP PCS results were declared too. Again, Avinash had been successful; he was selected for the post of accounts officer.

To celebrate his double success, he threw a party for his friends at Apni Rasoi restaurant right behind Batra Cinema. Manoj's new roommate, Sharad, asked Avinash, 'Bhaiya, what's the secret to your success? How did you prepare? Please give us some tips.'

'It's not so easy, Sharad. To learn from a guru, one has to show patience and work hard. The day success becomes a question of life and death for you, I'll share my secret. There are many who casually ask, but when I offer my advice, it goes in one ear and out the other,' said Avinash.

Sharad plucked up courage and asked again, 'How can you judge whether success is a question of life and death for someone?'

'One can easily see that you are yet to be serious about the exam. Every other month, you have to go to Gwalior to attend a cousin's wedding. How many cousins do you have?' Newfound success had boosted Avinash's confidence. He mercilessly attacked the newbie Sharad's casual attitude towards his studies.

Sharad had never thought that Avinash would judge him so harshly, and fell silent and returned to his soup. Manoj, on the other hand, suspected that something was lacking in his own preparation. He asked Avinash anxiously, 'Please tell us about your strategy. It will benefit us all.'

'Oh, there is nothing special. Come over sometime; we'll talk,' said Avinash, evading the question.

Pandey, listening to this discussion intently, took a slice of tomato from the plate of salad and said, 'Manoj is extremely busy these days. He doesn't have time for such useless things.'

Manoj's failure had brought immense satisfaction to Pandey as his prediction had come true. Naval was sitting opposite Pandey, sipping on a cold drink. Pandey said to him, 'Didn't I tell you that love will get him nowhere?' He was still holding Shraddha responsible for Manoj's failure. Though she was sitting right next to him, Pandey didn't care.

Avinash was in no mood to tolerate this nonsense while he was celebrating his success. 'Stop talking rubbish and focus on your manchurian,' he snapped. But this rebuke didn't deter

Pandey in the least. Manoj's failure had given him fresh energy. He sprang to his feet, pointed to Manoj and started rubbing salt in his wounds. 'Let's imagine that fifteen years down the line, you bump into Shraddha somewhere and she asks you, "What are you doing these days?" What will you say? "Shraddha, I work at a flour mill." Or, "I drive a tempo from Joura to Morena"?'

Manoj's face fell at his ex-roommate's spiteful comments. Shraddha was shocked and tears streamed down her cheeks. He didn't know what to do, and just looked at Pandey and Shraddha helplessly.

Avinash came to his rescue, 'Pandey, if you can't say something kind, better shut your mouth. What achievement do you have to boast of? You couldn't qualify for even the prelims. Manoj at least wrote the mains.'

But Pandey was immune to criticism and carried on while enjoying his manchurian. 'I am saying this for his own good. But I doubt he realizes this.' He wanted to help Manoj out by keeping him away from Shraddha. In his scheme of things, there was no place for her. Having humiliated them, he mixed the gravy of the manchurian with his fried rice and started eating it with great relish.

Feeling deeply insulted and embarrassed, Shraddha jumped to her feet, wiped her tears, and stormed out of the party. Manoj followed her. But that didn't stop Pandey from throwing the parting shot, 'It's no use crying over spilt milk.'

Manoj had faced humiliation on several occasions, including when his friends had mocked him in his village and when he had been accused of fraud at the library. For years, he had been subjected to indignities, barbs and taunts. But today, Pandey had put a question mark on his capability and his future, that too in Shraddha's presence. What's worse, he had held her responsible for Manoj's failure. They were walking down the road, their heads bent and went straight to a park in Mukherjee Nagar. 'I'll never forgive Pandey. Never, ever can I forget this insult,' said Manoj indignantly.

'Pandey has just held a mirror up to us,' said Shraddha, her voice calm. 'Success has many fathers, failure is an orphan—so get used to such insults now.' Saying this, she looked up to see Manoj's reaction. He was silent, his face flushed with anger and embarrassment.

Shraddha continued, 'Didn't I tell you time and again to study with single-minded determination! And throw everything else that distracts you out of the window. See, now people have started hurling insults at both of us.'

Stung by Pandey's biting remarks, Manoj had expected that Shraddha would sympathize with him and criticize Pandey. On the contrary, she had found fault with him. He burst out, 'What crime have I committed that I am being humiliated again and again? Now you are also blaming me.' His voice began to quaver. With his trembling hands, he gripped the bench Shraddha was sitting on. 'I'm not saying that you are wrong, Manoj,' she replied. 'But what's this talk again and again about love?'

Looking straight into her eyes, Manoj spluttered, 'Who do I love? What do I love?' He paused and added, 'Who loves me? You must know. If you do, why don't you tell me?' He stood up in a frenzy and then sat down again. 'I feel helpless. Is it my fault that I can't help thinking about you? Let others say whatever they want, I can't imagine a life without you. Love is not a strong enough word to express what I feel. You are in my every breath, every thought. Pandey was talking about only fifteen years. But I say whether it's fifteen or fifteen hundred, I'll wait for you.' Emotions that had been bottled up inside him for years came pouring out.

Shraddha's eyes rested on his face and Manoj averted his eyes. He paused, took a deep breath, and continued, 'Pandey says I'll never get through UPSC exam. Am I that weak? Does love weaken us? For me, it's enough to know that I came to your thoughts for even a moment. It gives me fresh energy to work. I can change the world, let alone get selected for IAS or IPS if only I have the strength of your love.'

Shraddha felt that he was not describing his state of mind, but hers. She had the same thoughts about Manoj. When he had gone off to his village, she longed for his company. Today, after listening to his outburst, her eyes were bright with unshed tears; she tried her best to hold them back. 'Let's go. We are getting late,' she said after a while. Manoj got up and walked with her silently. As he had already poured his heart out, he didn't have anything left to say. Shraddha, on the other hand, still seemed quite choked up, struggling to find the right words.

Outside her hostel, two girls were playing badminton under the street light. As they reached the hostel gate, Shraddha said, 'You have enormous potential, Manoj. If not, I wouldn't have said anything. If you don't make use of it, you will be committing a grave injustice to society. The sweetest way to take revenge on all those who have humiliated you will be to succeed in your aim and stand tall before them.'

It was time for Manoj to leave. The girls were still busy striking the shuttlecock. Looking at them, Shraddha said, 'I think of you all the time, not for a moment or two.' The memories of his five-day-long absence rushed to her mind. How restless she had grown for just a glimpse of him! Days of terrible loneliness and lassitude had become lively and joyous again when he returned. Shraddha turned her gaze away from the girls and looking deep into his eyes said, 'Manoj Sharma, I love you very much and will do so till my last breath.' There was complete silence between them, punctuated only by the shuttlecock hitting the racket. Shraddha didn't take her eyes off his face. After a pause, she added, 'Go now and change the world.' Then she turned and went into the hostel.

Manoj's world was changed. Her words were enough to spur him into action. They were still echoing in his ears: 'Go now and change the world.'

'You are not focusing on the shuttle. So, you lose the game every time. Watch it till the end,' one girl said to the other. Manoj heard them and a smile flickered across his face. Turning, he rushed to Gandhi Vihar instead of his room at Nehru Vihar. Since no autorickshaw was available, he broke into a run with a sudden burst of energy. His mind still replayed Shraddha's words: 'Manoj Sharma, I love you very much and will do so till my last breath.' He was dying to hear this one sentence again. He had waited for so long for Shraddha to reciprocate his love. Finally, it had happened. He felt he was not running but flying. Even plucking stars from the sky didn't seem impossible at that instant. Leaving his failure and disappointment behind, he raced in the pursuit of success, and in ten minutes, reached Avinash's room.

41

It was already 10 p.m. Avinash was astonished to see Manoj gasping for breath at his door. Without wasting a moment, Manoj said, 'I've got only one attempt remaining. I can't take any risk. Please help me.' Now the exam had become a question of life and death for Manoj, felt Avinash. Nevertheless, he said, 'You could have waited till tomorrow. Why did you take the trouble of coming so late at night?'

'The clock is ticking. For me, every second is precious,' came the reply.

Taking his digital watch off his wrist, Avinash said, 'Now that you are on the right track, please accept this gift.' Taken aback, Manoj replied, 'Thank you, but I don't need a gift. Kindly give me some useful tips for the exam.'

'Wear the watch first,' said Avinash with a smile.

Manoj strapped the digital watch on his wrist without saying a word. Avinash pressed a button on the watch, and said, 'I'll tell you some basic rules of study. This is a stopwatch. I have started it. The watch will tell us precisely how much time we spend on talking. Your time starts now.' He added, 'The prelims will be held on 22 May, that's one month from now. You have to focus on that; forget about the mains.'

Then he said, 'Go through the previous years' question papers meticulously. In the prelims, several questions are asked directly from there. Owing to our negligence, we often fail to answer them. Try to solve thousands of objective questions from the practice book and don't take any part of the syllabus lightly.' Manoj jotted down all of Avinash's suggestions.

'You should follow the same strategy for the general studies paper,' Avinash continued. 'Yes, these days, a large number of questions are based on current affairs. Any monthly magazine will help you solve them.'

Avinash paused the stopwatch, and said, 'Look, I spoke precisely for ten minutes sixteen seconds.' He asked Manoj, 'How many hours do you study daily?'

'Approximately ten,' said Manoj, hesitating for a moment.

'Are you sure?' Avinash asked, smiling.

Manoj remained silent. He had never counted his hours of study.

'From now on you have to keep track of every minute,' said Avinash. 'So, wear this stopwatch all the time. While reading turn it on, but when you take a break to eat or talk, pause it. Note down the number of hours you study in a day as per the watch. Eight hours is poor, ten good and twelve is very good. This will motivate you.'

Manoj had never kept count of the number of hours he studied. As long as the book lay open before him, he assumed that he had studied for ten hours, even if he was actually chatting with his roommate. He left for his room enthusiastically and the next day, he discussed his new strategy with Shraddha.

'Avinash has given you the right advice,' she said. 'I've made up my mind to concentrate on Uttarakhand PSC. This year, I won't appear for the IAS exam, but for you, it's now or never. I want to see my Manoj join the IPS.'

Initially, as per the stopwatch, Manoj studied for just about six hours. This moved to twelve gradually. With the right strategy and diligence, his preparation for the prelims had become adequate in a month. Shraddha asked him to quit his job as a dog walker to save time and study with complete dedication. To support him, she decided to reduce her expenses by sharing her room with a girl. Somehow, she could manage to save Rs 1,000 to help Manoj pay his rent.

42

Manoj did well in the prelims. Shraddha had appeared in the Uttarakhand PCS exam. The day following the prelims, Vikas Sir invited Sourav Rao—who had got through the UPSC exam last year in the Hindi medium—to his institute. Manoj wanted to follow a coherent strategy to get through the mains, so he listened to Rao intently. Then he asked, 'Sir, what should one do to score well in the mains?'

'It's difficult, but not impossible. You must remember that in the mains, you have to write subjective answers and therefore, your strategy must be different from that of the prelims. It's better to mug up as much as you can and practise writing answers simultaneously. Solve the previous years' papers and participate in mock tests,' replied Sourav. The session was enlightening for Manoj.

'Now I realize why I failed in my third attempt; I used to mug up notes, but never worked on improving my writing skills. Nor did I take mock tests. Merely cramming facts won't do. We should write down many times over whatever we memorize. From now on, I'll follow Sourav Sir's advice,' he told Shraddha.

They walked up to Shakti Pustak Bhandar in Mukherjee Nagar, where Manoj bought two bundles of 500 blank sheets and said, 'In one month, we have to finish them, which means roughly twenty pages a day. You should also do the same for your state PSC. Now, let's write twenty pages every day. First we'll mug up, then write, and finally take the test. This routine will continue till our exams get over.' However, he was still worried. 'There is a problem, Shraddha,' he said. 'What if I can't write well?'

'That can be tackled,' she replied. 'Students decide to write only after perfecting their skills, and many end up writing answers for the first time in the exam hall. It's better to practise and improve one's poor skills at home than to write terrible answers in the exam.'

'I agree with you. In the next few months, I'll write more than I've written in my entire life,' decided Manoj.

He started waking up at 4 a.m. He would go through the old question papers, memorize the important topics from the notes and books, and then write down his answers within a specified time. From morning to noon and—after a two-hour break for lunch and a siesta—from two in the afternoon to six in the evening, the same exercise was repeated. Unlike when he was preparing for his third attempt, Shraddha no longer came to his room in the morning. Rather, she set the entire day's target for him, and reached around six in the evening with handwritten notes on science and technology, international relations and current affairs that she had prepared during the day. They mugged up several topics of general studies and scribbled down the main points till ten at night.

General studies still posed a challenge for Manoj, making him realize that it was impossible to get good marks in this paper without joining a coaching institute. One day, Shraddha told him that her friend had joined Dhyeya Coaching Centre started recently by Vinay Sir, a highly competent teacher. They went together to Dhyeya and Shraddha broached the subject, 'Sir, we want to join your classes, but don't have enough money; only one of us will be able to pay.' Vinay Singh had to encounter a student in his very first batch who couldn't afford the fee.

Manoj pleaded honestly, 'Sir, I have no money at all, but it will do me a world of good if you let me prepare under your guidance.'

Only fifteen students had joined the coaching so far. Vinay needed more students, but he didn't want to entertain a freeloader. So, he tried to dissuade him, saying, 'If I teach you without taking fee, it'll be an injustice to others.'

But Manoj persisted, 'Sir, I'll never get through the mains without proper coaching. I promise once I clear the exam and get my first salary, I'll pay your fee.'

Vinay Sir just laughed and pulled out Rs 8,000 from the drawer. He gave the notes to Manoj and said, 'I can't waive off your fee. So take this and deposit it at that counter. When you have money, return it to me. But I can't deprive you of coaching just because you can't afford it.'

An unknown teacher had generously helped him with Rs 8,000 at the very first meeting; Manoj's heart overflowed with gratitude.

Vinay Singh's teaching method was quite exam-oriented. There was an emphasis on mock tests in his class. Every day, before starting his lecture, he conducted a test to make sure that students had learnt whatever had been taught the previous day.

Manoj continued to work towards his target of writing down hundreds of answers in Hindi, history and general studies. Both his teachers, Vikas and Vinay, evaluated his answers regularly and suggested ways to improve them. He followed their suggestions with the utmost sincerity.

On 5 August, Avinash threw a party at his room to celebrate his birthday. Since Manoj was satisfied with the progress of his studies, he also joined the party and was dancing wildly. Gupta and Sharad were dancing too. Although Manoj's movements were out of rhythm, Shraddha was delighted to see his unique steps. Meanwhile, Naval and Pandey were busy chopping onions and tomatoes for paneer curry.

At that moment, someone broke the news that the results of the prelims were out. The music stopped, the dancers froze and their hearts raced. Manoj slumped to the floor. Despite feeling that he had done the exam well, he dreaded the results. What if he failed to qualify in his last attempt? Halved onions and tomatoes lay in the kitchen. Pandey, Avinash, Gupta, Naval and Manoj were nervous about the results; only Sharad stood calmly since he hadn't taken the exam.

They sent him to check the results on the internet. He returned with the news that everyone had cleared the prelims except Gupta, who let out a cry of despair. Then he took a deep drag of his cigarette, closed his eyes and collapsed on the floor. Everyone panicked. Shaking him vigorously, Avinash said, 'What happened? Come on, get up.' Sharad splashed his face with cold water and Gupta returned to his senses. He retreated to his room and bolted the door. All his four attempts were now over and he hadn't cleared the prelims even once.

His friends got a bit concerned and gathered outside the room. Avinash called out, 'Gupta, stop the drama and step out. Onions and tomatoes have been chopped. Who will cook the paneer?' Gupta was an excellent cook, so the responsibility of preparing food lay on his shoulders. Today, the group had registered a much higher ratio of success. Avinash was in no mood to cancel the party only because one of them was sulking. But despite his persuasion, Gupta didn't respond. Even though the tension in the room grew, Avinash was more bothered about who would cook the paneer curry.

Naval consoled Gupta, 'So what if all of your attempts are gone? In the state PCS exam, there is no such restriction. You can appear for it till you turn forty. You still have ten more years. Don't lose hope.' He kicked the door, perhaps warning Gupta that if he didn't step out soon, the door could be broken open. Gupta also didn't want to test the patience of his friends for long. He feared that if he continued to sulk they might leave him alone and go off to Apni Rasoi restaurant to dine out. Then there wouldn't be anyone left to coax him.

So, he relented and stepped out with two epaulettes—bearing a stainless steel 'IPS' and three stars each—that he had torn off the khaki uniform he had bought to inspire himself to become a police officer. He flung them into the dustbin and exclaimed, 'Fuck it! I am relieved that the farce is over. Anyway, in IPS it's hard to get a posting in your home state. There is no point becoming an IPS officer in Kerala or West Bengal. Who has seen the dance of a peacock in the jungle?'

Manoj pulled out the epaulettes from the dustbin and put them into his pocket. After a few days, they learnt that Shraddha had cleared the Uttarakhand PCS prelims and she went to Haridwar to write the mains, while Manoj resumed his preparation with renewed enthusiasm.

Day and night, he sweated and swotted. The target of writing down twenty pages per day went up to thirty. A strange obsession seized him. He forgot everything else—his home, family, friends and relatives—except intensive reading and writing. The mains were only a month away. He continued to appear for the mock tests at the coaching centre. For three hours, he would take the test with absolute determination. Before writing down his answers, he always made a rough sketch of the major points he was going to elaborate on. Even if it took him more than five minutes to prepare the sketch, he never started his answer without it. Within a month, he took some thirty mock tests, which enhanced his confidence manifold.

Manoj's exam centre was in Delhi and with their exams over, Shraddha and Manoj anxiously waited for the results of both Uttarakhand PSC and UPSC mains.

43

Sharad again went to an internet café to check the results, while Avinash, Naval and Pandey waited with bated breath in Manoj's room. It was Pandey's first mains. Forgetting past animosity, he had come to Manoj's room as well. Equally eager to learn what the future held for Manoj was Shraddha. The first round of exams had separated the grain from the chaff and Gupta was out of the race. Now, free from all anxieties, he awaited today's results with amusement. Making good use of this time, he assumed the role of a journalist and, puffing away at a cigarette, said, 'Manojji, this is your last attempt. How do you feel?'

Avinash abused him and said, 'Gupta, my heart is in my mouth and you are asking nonsensical questions.'

But Manoj played along and replied, 'I know this is my last attempt. That is why I have put my heart and soul into the preparation. I've given my best; the rest is not in my hands.'

At that instant, Sharad came in, panting after running up the steps. Everyone's heart skipped a beat. Without keeping anyone in suspense, he broke the news at once. 'Manoj bhaiya and Avinashji have cleared the mains. Pandey and Naval haven't.'

Manoj couldn't believe his ears; he had got through the first mains exam of his life. He wanted to let out a shriek of delight, but looking at the crestfallen faces of Pandey and Naval, kept his emotions in check. They sank into despair and Gupta now had two new partners to share his grief. He was content to see that his ilk was expanding.

'You shouldn't lose heart. In your next attempt, you'll certainly succeed.' Manoj tried to comfort them, but it was of no use. Pandey slumped into bed, listless, and Naval sat on a chair shedding tears. It was a dramatic scene: two successful people were elated, the two unsuccessful ones were disconsolate, and two observers—with no stakes whatsoever—were congratulating the former and commiserating with the latter.

Everyone left after a while. On the way out, Gupta said to Avinash, 'You always said that those who prepare for civil services shouldn't fall in love. But today, Manoj, who is madly in love, succeeded, while Pandey, who is miles away from love, failed. What do you have to say now?'

'Nothing. Just shut up and walk,' Avinash replied, in irritation. He didn't want to hurt Pandey by speaking on this sensitive subject. Pandey was deeply upset by his failure, unable to figure out how Manoj got through the mains. He had no clue about the strategy his ex-roommate adopted in the last five months. Gupta, on the other hand, was unaffected by the result, so he continued to comment without any inhibition. 'Manoj must be over the moon as he got both love as well as success. Do you know, Avinash, what's the best decision of his life?' Gupta was not only analysing the outcome of the exam but also wanted to win Avinash's approval.

'Okay, go on,' said Avinash. 'I know you can't be silent; you have to share what's going on in your mind.'

'Throwing Pandey out of his room and falling in love with Shraddha,' said Gupta, lowering his voice to a whisper. As soon as Pandey heard this, his eyes blazed with anger. He exploded, 'Gupta, let me tell you first that Manoj never forced me to leave his room. I was the one who left him. Second, he hasn't achieved anything as yet; this is not the final result. He is yet to clear the interview. And third, I've seen several such lovers. The day Shraddha's parents get to know that instead of focusing on studies, she is in love with some boy, they will drag her away and Manoj will be left watching helplessly.'

'But who will tell her parents?' Gupta asked.

Pandey's mind was assailed by many emotions: anger, sorrow, jealousy, disappointment and a sense of defeat. He was getting out of control, unable to stomach the news of Manoj's success. 'Someone may tell them. For how long such things can be concealed? The days of his love story are numbered,' he screamed, and stomped away furiously.

44

Now that Manoj's neighbour Varun had exhausted all his attempts at the UPSC exam, he spent his evenings chanting the Hanuman Chalisa. After a few days of the declaration of results, Manoj went to his room. On seeing his beaming face, Varun said, 'You are still far from success. Look at me. I've appeared for the interview twice, but what happened at the end? I am still stuck where I started from. All my four attempts are over. How shall I face my parents? That's why I am staying here. Prelims, mains, interview—all are illusions. Until your name appears in the final list of selected candidates, you've no right to be happy.'

Varun had poured out his frustration and advised him to be realistic. Manoj silently returned to his room.

My feelings oscillate between hope and despair. How many people can realize their dreams? How many aspirants get selected in the exam? Three hundred out of lakhs. The rest get rejected. They lose heart and weep bitterly, with no confidence left to look anyone in the eye for many days. After a break, they begin to identify their shortcomings and seek to remedy them. And then starts the process of going through the same notes. This continues year after year until one among thousands reaches his destination. Zillions of others end in failure. This is an endless process that plagues not only Mukherjee Nagar but every nook and corner of India.

Manoj penned all these thoughts down in his diary. While he was reflecting on his forthcoming interview and the uncertainty of its outcome, Shraddha came in and broke the news. Brimming with confidence, she said, 'I have got through the Uttarakhand mains.'

Manoj was thrilled to hear this. 'Hats off to you on this success!' he exclaimed.

She took his hands into hers and said, 'Our interviews are yet to happen, Manoj.'

'You'll outperform everyone else in the interview,' he said excitedly. 'Nothing can stop you now from becoming a deputy collector.'

'If I become one, how ecstatic my father would be! His dream will come true. I'll be able to hold my head high before him. He was extremely disappointed when I couldn't get admission in MBBS.' She added, 'I'm leaving for Almora. From there, I'll go to Haridwar with my father to face the interview and then return to Delhi.'

'Please come back soon. I'll wait for you,' Manoj pleaded.

'I'll be back before your interview. But you better focus on your preparations until then.' She left for Almora the next day.

One day, Shraddha called him on the telephone booth located on the ground floor of his building and said, 'My interview went off well.' And after a pause she added, 'But I won't be able to come to Delhi anytime soon.'

'Why, what happened?' Manoj asked, surprised.

'An anonymous caller from Delhi told Papa that his daughter was in love with a boy,' said Shraddha, her voice low. 'Mummy tells me that Papa is very upset.'

'Who do you think called him?' asked a bewildered Manoj.

'How would I know?' She too couldn't think of a suspect.

Manoj felt sad and returned to his room. Some five days later, Shraddha called up again. 'I've been selected for the post of deputy collector!' she chirped.

His joy knew no bounds. 'Wah, Shraddha!' he exclaimed. 'This is excellent news. God has showered us with His blessings today.'

'Yes, I'm delighted. I've fulfilled my father's dream today. He is thrilled,' said Shraddha.

'So am I. Thrilled to bits. You'll return to Delhi before my interview. Won't you?' Her success suddenly reminded him of his upcoming interview.

'Ever since he got that anonymous call from Delhi, papa thinks I've breached his trust,' she said, her voice tinged with sadness.

'So the only way to win one's parents' trust is to stop being in love?' asked Manoj gravely.

Shraddha remained silent.

45

It had been quite some time now since the mains results had been declared. Pandey's anger and sorrow were beginning to drain away. One evening, when Avinash was leaving for Manoj's room, he also went along. Varun was reciting Hanuman Chalisa. But he sounded low today. By the time he reached the lines '*Vidyavan guni ati chatur, Ram kaaj karibe ko atur*', his voice quavered and he started weeping. Then, all of a sudden, a clatter was heard from his room as if someone was banging metal on the floor.

Manoj, Pandey and Avinash rushed to his room, and found Varun sitting on the bed and crying loudly. The brass statue of Lord Hanuman, His throne, and other gods and goddesses lay strewn on the floor near the almirah where he kept them. Everyone panicked. They suspected that some tragedy had befallen Varun's family. His roommate cowered in a corner. Manoj asked him the reason for Varun's wailing. But before he could respond, Varun shrieked, 'Vandana, Vandana, where have you gone? How will I live without you?'

It didn't take the others long to realize that a girl was the source of his grief. As soon as Varun's roomie got a chance, he narrated the incident at length. 'Varun's girlfriend got selected for the post of sales tax inspector in the UP PSC exam. He had fallen in love with her when they were preparing for the exam. The girl had promised to marry him once he got a job. She got through, Varun hadn't. So she married someone else who had become a DSP in UP. The news has left Varun devastated.'

Having consoled Varun, they stepped out of his room. 'Career should always be one's top priority. One has all the time in the world to fall in love,' said Pandey and looked at Manoj, as if these words were directed at him. He added with a chuckle, 'Avinash, in Varun, I can see Manoj's future. Take my word: whether you get the girl or not depends on you getting a job. Suppose he doesn't clear the interview, and Shraddha who is a deputy collector now, leaves him? What will he do?'

'Shraddha is a sensible girl. She won't go anywhere,' Avinash replied judiciously.

'Sensible girls are the ones who move on to greener pastures. Stupid ones get stuck with one person. Shraddha is sensible and that's the main problem. Varun's Vandana was also sensible, so she chose a DSP groom for herself. If she were stupid, she would have ruined her life with Varun.' Pandey had absolute trust in Shraddha's wisdom, and enormous confidence in his belief that if Manoj failed she would drop him.

'Manoj will surely get selected. You are doubting his abilities for no reason,' said Avinash.

'Don't talk nonsense!' Pandey didn't give up. 'Be realistic. What's the guarantee of his success? All 1,500 candidates appearing for the interview must be thinking the same. But how many will get through? Only 500. The rest will be weeded out. Suppose Manoj does not get selected and Shraddha goes away from his life, he will be finished.'

But Manoj had complete trust in her. 'You don't know her well enough. She'll never leave the person she has chosen for herself,' he said.

'Every lover entertains such a fantasy. Varun also thought the same,' Pandey shot back.

Turning his eyes to Avinash, he added, 'She should have come to Manoj immediately after becoming a deputy collector. It has been more than a week since the results were declared, but she is nowhere in sight. Now she is waiting for his results. If he succeeds, she will come, and if he doesn't, she will vanish into thin air. Shraddha will become Vandana in no time.'

46

A few days after his mock interview, when Manoj returned from the coaching centre, he saw Varun leaving with a suitcase. 'Where are you going, Varun bhai?' he asked.

'This unfaithful city doesn't suit me. I'm leaving for home. So what if I couldn't become an IAS officer? I'm not dead yet! Anyway, what groundbreaking work have the government officers done? All they can do is go licking the boots of politicians. So, I'll join politics now and become a minister. Don't lose hope if you can't clear the interview. Join my party; I'll make you an MLA,' he said.

Varun looked unkempt—his eyes were red, he had neither shaved nor slept properly for many days. Like a madman he rambled on and on. He seemed restless and fidgety. Forgetting his suitcase on the floor, he moved on towards the stairs, but on realizing his mistake, he returned to pick it up. While climbing down, he stumbled and fell on the last few steps. The suitcase burst open, his ex-girlfriend Vandana's photos and some of his clothes fell out. Manoj rushed to his help and stuffed everything back into the suitcase. Varun turned and said, his gazed fixed on his room, 'Five long years I've stayed here. Never, ever will I come back to this place!' He hugged Manoj and started weeping. Manoj too couldn't hold back his tears. Shortly afterwards, Varun took a rickshaw and went away. Manoj stood watching him until he was out of sight.

47

After getting through the PSC exam with flying colours, Shraddha was keen to get back to Delhi before Manoj's interview. But because of the anonymous call, she hesitated to broach this subject with her father. One day, she saw him watering the plants in the garden. 'Papa, the roses are in full bloom. Last year, they had wilted without water.' She gathered the courage to start a conversation.

'We have planted roses this year. Last year, we didn't have them in our garden. Perhaps you want to say something else.' Her father understood her dilemma.

Shraddha still couldn't bring herself to talk about Manoj. But without seeking her father's permission, she couldn't go back to Delhi. Her father had never raised the issue of the anonymous phone call before her. She had got to know about it from her mother. Finally, she made up her mind to broach the subject. 'Papa, Manoj is in Delhi,' she fumbled for words and couldn't make eye contact with him.

She stood there, a lump rising in her throat. Looking at her face flushed with embarrassment, he could read her mind and asked, 'Did he also become a deputy collector like you?'

Answering his questions was no easy task. 'He has cleared the UPSC mains. The interview is yet to take place,' she said.

'Which attempt was this?' he enquired.

'Last,' replied Shraddha, her head bent.

Following a moment of silence, she said, 'Papa, Manoj has to appear for the interview in a few days. Can I go to Delhi?'

'Let him get through it first.' Her father's approach was pragmatic.

'Papa, if he doesn't get selected, it will become all the more important to be with him,' she said, summoning up her courage.

Her father was lost for words. However, after a pause, he said firmly, 'I hope you won't breach my trust.'

'So the only way to win one's parents' trust is to stop being in love?' This was what Manoj had told her earlier. She wanted to ask the same question, but couldn't utter a word. Feeling helpless, she went to her room, her eyes filled with tears.

Soon thereafter, a felicitation ceremony was organized in her old school, Saraswati Shishu Mandir, to celebrate her success. Her parents were also invited to sit on the dais with her. The principal presented her with a medal and requested her to say a few words to encourage the children. Shraddha began her address, 'Respected principal, teachers, and my dear sisters and brothers, a similar felicitation ceremony was held here some seven years ago to honour the alumni of this institution who had got admitted into the MBBS course. Having failed to clear the medical entrance, I was sitting at the back, disheartened. My father always trusted my ability to achieve something big in life, but I had disappointed him.'

She took a deep breath and continued, 'That day, I promised myself that I'll never let him down, no matter what. Dear students, it doesn't matter what goal we set for ourselves. What truly matters is whether or not we put our heart and soul into achieving it. We should promise ourselves, our parents and friends that we won't stop till the goal is reached.'

She stopped and thought for a moment. All the parents in the auditorium were listening to her with rapt attention. Turning her eyes to them, she added, 'But parents also must tell their children, "If you don't succeed despite giving your best, you can always lean on us for support. It's alright to fail. Work hard with renewed zeal; victory will be yours. We will stand by you through thick and thin."'

Shraddha reached the concluding part of her speech. 'Children expect love and support of their friends and family even more when they stumble and fall. Your reassurance and affection will work wonders, and they will eventually get success because every cloud has a silver lining.'

Having finished her speech, she sat down to huge applause, her words still echoing in her father's mind.

Manoj's interview was only two days away. With her eyes shut, Shraddha lay in bed that night, clutching her diary to her chest. Tears lay dried on her cheeks. A few drops had smudged some pages in her diary. Her father entered her room and picked it up, but couldn't figure out what she had written because it was so smudged. He placed it under her pillow and looked intently at her. The girl who had fulfilled Papa's dream a few days back appeared so dejected today. Who understood Shraddha better than her Papa? She was his darling daughter. He had complete faith in her judgement. She never pestered him for anything. Nor did she express any specific wish. She always focused on her studies.

Memories came flooding back to him. He recalled the day when she had worn her school uniform for the first time. The three-year-old tiny Shraddha was so unwilling to go to school. She just wanted to play with her rabbit, Cheeku, that he had gifted her. However, she never insisted that she wouldn't go to school. Her eyes turned to Cheeku time and again; her face fell. Papa had picked her up and climbed up the steps of Mall Road. He felt the drops of her warm tears on his cheek, but when he looked at her, a faint smile flickered across her face. Perhaps little Shraddha was trying to hide her tears in the guise of smile.

Today, when she opened her eyes and found Papa looking at her, she did the same— she managed a weak smile. He sat down and gently stroked her forehead. An ocean of tears welled up in her blue eyes. Papa hugged her and all the anxieties oppressing her for the past few days melted away. The frightened sparrow felt alive and was ready to take off again.

48

Manoj's interview was only one day away. He was still anxiously waiting for Shraddha to return from Almora. He had taken coaching from Vikas Sir and thoroughly prepared himself for answering questions on his educational background, hometown and current affairs. But questions one never expected could be asked. So what should he read now? Puzzled, he opened his diary—the story of his life's arduous journey, the tale of a twelfth-fail boy who was about to face the UPSC interview.

Flipping through the pages, he recalled the day Pandey had taken him to Tyagiji and helped him get a job; the day Pandey had come to the flour mill and asked him to come along and stay in Peelikothi. If he had reached till the interview, much of the credit should go to Pandey. He felt immensely grateful to his old friend and felt a strong urge to meet him.

As soon as he stepped out of his room to leave for Gandhi Vihar, he saw Shraddha walking towards him with long strides, her eyes alight with excitement and face wreathed in smiles. In her absence, he felt empty, but her very presence made him feel newly alive. Life suddenly seemed to be back on track. 'Sorry, I couldn't come earlier,' said Shraddha.

With a radiant smile, Manoj responded, 'You've arrived at the right moment. Ever since you entered my life, things have turned out well.'

A shy smile spread across her face on listening to this generous compliment. Manoj added, 'I've to go to meet Pandey. I can never forget his contribution to my life. Without his generous support, perhaps I wouldn't have come so far.'

'But he humiliated you!' she exclaimed.

'He is still my friend. I can't forget his help during those days when I was struggling in Gwalior. Shraddha, I had read an essay titled "Five Nuggets of Harpal Singh" in class five, which left a lasting impression on me. It was mentioned there that we should never abandon the person who supported us when we faced a crisis.'

Shraddha's eyes misted over with tears. 'I am so glad that I've chosen the best man in the world as my life partner. A man with a heart of gold, who loves everyone. Such a person can never hate anyone,' she said.

'When your heart is filled with deep love for someone, there is no room for hatred,' responded Manoj.

They reached Pandey's room in Gandhi Vihar and found him lying in bed, humming a song: '*Dukhi man mere sun mera kehna, jahan nahin chaina whan nahin rehna*'. He was surprised to see Shraddha with Manoj and sprang to his feet. 'Tomorrow is my interview,' Manoj told him. 'Except Shraddha, if someone has ever helped me, it's you. Without your support, I wouldn't have reached here. I need your best wishes for tomorrow.'

Shraddha joined him, saying, 'Bhaiya, you must make an all-out effort in your last attempt. Look at Manoj. He got a call for the interview in his last chance.'

'What if he is not selected?' Pandey tried to gauge her feelings. He still believed that she would cut Manoj out of her life if he didn't get through. But Shraddha proved him wrong. 'What matters most is he has put in a great deal of effort. Now, if he fails, there are plenty of other opportunities. For me, Manoj is important, not what he becomes.' While saying the last sentence, she lowered her eyes.

'Pandey, don't leave any stone unturned this year,' said Manoj, encouraging him. 'You'll see how all your doubts are swept away. It's your hard work that keeps negativity at bay and ensures success.'

All of Pandey's efforts to separate Manoj from Shraddha had failed. He decided to reconcile with the changed circumstances. His heart felt light on getting their reassurances and consolations. After chatting for a while, he walked them till the Gandhi Vihar autorickshaw stand. While they were waiting for an autorickshaw, he got carried away and said, 'Manoj, I had called up Shraddha's father.'

'It's alright. If this is what God wished, so be it!' Manoj said.

They left in an autorickshaw as Pandey watched them silently.

49

Manoj and Shraddha got ready to leave for the UPSC office. It was the very first interview of his life. 'I feel scared,' he said. 'God knows what all they will ask. I wonder if I'll be able to answer them correctly. So many topics remained untouched; I couldn't do the revision properly.'

'Just remember one thing. The purpose of this interview is to assess your personality, to know the kind of person you are, how you view life, society, our country and the world, and most importantly, this job. So, you don't have to revise anything but know yourself.' Shraddha then shared her experiences of the PSC interview.

Candidates swarmed the gate of the UPSC office. Everyone was in formal dress—boys clad in off-white shirt, and navy-blue blazers and trousers, and the girls draped in saris. Their admit cards were being checked at gate number one. Friends and relatives who had accompanied them entered through a different gate and waited in the park. After wishing Manoj good luck, Shraddha also joined them.

All the candidates entered a big hall where officials verified their markssheets and other documents. Pictures of Mahatma Gandhi and Sardar Patel were hung on the wall. At 10 a.m. sharp, the hall sprang to life. Guards moved all around. The candidates knew that the experts had come. Their heart began pounding and throats became dry.

Manoj's interview would be taken by a board chaired by Dr P.D. Mehta, the former director of Indian Institute of Technology (IIT) Delhi, currently serving as a member of UPSC. The news disheartened him as the chairman of his board had nothing to do with Hindi literature or history. Moreover, Dr Mehta was known for his preferential treatment to engineering and English-medium students, and for his bias against those from the social sciences and Hindi-medium backgrounds.

The peon came and called out the name of the first candidate. The others grew a little tense as the young man went into the room. Twenty minutes later, he emerged with a long face and shared his experience with others, 'When I told them doing yoga is my hobby and that I've been practising it ever since I was in class ten, Chairman Mehta glared at me and said, "You eat daily. Does it mean that eating is your hobby too?" I couldn't say anything. He looked intimidating and solemn; doesn't even smile.'

When the next student came out, he appeared equally disappointed. Dr Mehta pulled him up for his low marks in his BSc physics. He grilled him for some twenty minutes and, at the end, advised him to come better prepared next time. Holding back tears, the young man walked away. Manoj got rattled when he heard these accounts. He shivered when he recalled his past failures—third division in class ten; twelfth fail with a zero in mathematics, physics and chemistry; and second division in BA with an abysmally poor score in English literature. Dr Mehta would chew him out. The thought alarmed Manoj.

Meanwhile, the third candidate emerged with a beaming face, and announced that he had done really well. He had studied at IIT Delhi and was working as a software engineer at Infosys. His entire interview revolved around the use of information technology in administration. Dr Mehta complimented him on his excellent answers many times. This was bad news for Manoj too, whose knowledge of information technology was limited to his notes.

He closed his eyes to calm his nerves and assuage his fears. The story of his whole life rapidly unfolded before him—his village, his home, the college in Gwalior, the library, and Shraddha waiting for him outside. His name was called out. He rose to his feet, ran his fingers through his hair, adjusted his eyeglasses and walked into the room. The long-awaited moment had at last come.

Inside, there was a U-shaped table behind which five experts were seated—an elderly man in a dhoti-kurta and four others in suits. Manoj greeted them and stood near the chair kept for the candidate. Dr Mehta, who was at the centre, motioned him to sit down.

Manoj thanked him and took his seat. All the members of the board were smiling. Perhaps they were trying to put him at ease. Since they knew that an aspirant was generally nervous at the start of the interview, the initial questions were basic and introductory. 'Well, Manoj, why do you want to join the civil services? What inspired you to join the administration?' asked Dr Mehta.

The question was simple. One didn't require any great expertise to answer it. However, Manoj thought for a few seconds. The image of Dushyant Singh, SDM of Joura, popped into his mind. He answered, 'Sir, I used to run a tempo. Once the police seized it. I went to meet Dushyant Sir. His sincerity, honesty and his the ability to take swift action inspired me. Since then I wanted to join the civil services.'

Dr Mehta was not satisfied with this answer. 'Everyone who comes here narrates such stories. But the truth is that through this service you want to enjoy power, privilege and high status in society,' he said curtly.

It unnerved Manoj to see the chairman dismiss his life's story as something cooked up. Suddenly a question so simple appeared complicated. The members didn't have a machine to distinguish truth from falsehood! He couldn't have torn his chest open like Hanuman to show what lay in his heart, so he remained silent. Dr Mehta gave the signal to the other member, who was engrossed in Manoj's file, to ask questions.

'A second division in both twelfth and BA, and a third division in tenth. You've been academically very weak,' he commented, reading through the file. Suddenly, his eyes were drawn to an entry that prompted him to ask abruptly, 'Oh, it took you two years to pass the twelfth exam. Why did this happen?'

Manoj's worst fears had come true. His past failure in the twelfth board exam confronted him once again like a demon. Either it would devour him or he would vanquish it. Fortunately for him, he hadn't got out of the habit of taking on a challenge fearlessly. His mind raced, trying to think of ways to dodge this unpleasant question. All sorts of excuses came flooding into his mind—'Sir, my grandfather had passed away that year. I fell ill on the day of the exam.' No one believed him when he spoke the truth. He thought of telling a lie for a moment, but finally decided to tell the truth. Somehow, he felt that truth was the only force that could save him.

'Sir, I had failed in all the subjects except Hindi because cheating wasn't allowed that year in the school,' he answered, his voice remarkably composed. He had no idea what effect this shocking revelation would have on the members. They would either appreciate the truth or show him the door at once.

Dr Mehta had seen some of the brightest minds of the country in the IITs, who had been toppers throughout their career. He considered such gems the future of India, driven by the belief that the administration could be smoothly run only by English-medium students. But it surprised him that a twelfth-fail boy had limped his way to this stage, sitting pretty confidently before the board. Manoj's reply stunned him. He could never imagine that someone would ever give such a stupid answer in an interview. Suddenly, Manoj came across as an unfit candidate for the civil services. He himself had exposed the chink in his armour to Dr Mehta, who glared at him and said, 'You wanted to cheat in the exam? We've never met a student who brazenly admits that he wanted to pass an exam through cheating.'

God knows from where Manoj got such confidence that he remained unfazed by this unsettling comment. Rather, he looked him straight in the eye and said, 'Sir, please go to Bhind and Morena sometime, and pay a visit to the government schools. Even today, students pass the exam through cheating. Is it their fault or does the fault lie with the system that can't discipline them? Once, Dushyant Singh didn't let anyone cheat and most of them failed. But one such student is sitting before you by dint of his hard work. Had Dushyant Sir not stopped students from adopting unfair means that year, perhaps I would have never understood the value of education.'

Members of the board seemed impressed with his answer. They started talking to one another in agreement, but Dr Mehta continued without budging, 'Whatever you may say, I've seen your entire career graph. You are very weak at English; you have barely managed to pass in it. The administration can't be run by someone who doesn't possess a good command over English.'

Manoj was trapped once more. Dr Mehta couldn't be swayed so easily. But Manoj too stood his ground. 'Sir, in the administration, language is not as important as right intentions,' he said.

Dr Mehta wasn't happy to see a newbie challenge his belief on the importance of English. 'No, this is just an excuse to hide your shortcomings. How can you serve the country if your English is poor?' he asked indignantly. What irony! Dr Mehta was speaking in English to a candidate who had admitted his weak grasp of the language. Manoj tried to understand the question, but groped for words. English had become a thorn in his side again. Beads of sweat formed on his forehead. The elderly member clad in the dhoti-kurta noticed his nervous face and said, gesturing towards the glass kept on the table, 'Would you like to have some water?'

Manoj saw the glass, but didn't have the courage to drink. Silence fell over the room for a few seconds. A smile of satisfaction played across Dr Mehta's lips. He was having fun inflicting wounds on Manoj with the weapon of English. His eyes fixed on the glass, Manoj thought for a while and then picked it up. 'Sir, I can't drink this water,' he said abruptly. Everyone was baffled by his behaviour.

'Is it dirty, Manoj?' one member asked.

'No, sir. The water is clean, but I don't drink from a glass. I prefer a steel tumbler,' he politely answered.

Dr Mehta didn't get him and asked in a rather annoyed tone, 'Is that some kind of joke? If you want to drink water, why do you bother about the tumbler? Water will remain the same no matter what contains it.'

Manoj answered amicably, 'That is precisely what I want to say. The important thing is the water and not the container. If the water is clean, it doesn't matter whether it's in a glass or in a steel tumbler. If your thoughts, emotions and ideas are good and in the interests of the nation, it doesn't matter whether you express them in Hindi or English.'

Saying this, he gulped down the water and put the glass back on the table. His response took all the members by surprise. The face of the elderly member lit up. 'Wah, Manoj!' he exclaimed.

Dr Mehta was still poring over the certificates. English, his sharpest weapon, had been blunted by Manoj's answer, but he was not going to let him off the hook so easily. This time, he turned to other members and asked, 'You all have seen the IIT graduate who came before Manoj. He was a state topper in the twelfth exam. In place of him, why should we select someone who once failed in the twelfth?'

All the members seemed to agree with the chairman. Turning towards Manoj, the elderly member asked, 'Yes, why should we prefer you to a state topper?'

The spectre of his failure in the twelfth exam kept haunting him. His entire interview seemed to revolve around it. All the incidents of national and international importance that he had prepared were of no use because Dr Mehta had made up his mind to attack him for his past failures. The board had compared a twelfth-fail student with one of the brightest students of India. But Manoj was determined not to concede defeat. 'Because I am more capable than him,' he replied, declaring himself better than an IIT graduate.

With an air of bemused disbelief, the experts started looking at one another. One of them then asked, 'How can you call yourself better than the boy who has topped in every class since his childhood?'

Manoj answered, 'The greatest strength of an individual lies in overcoming one's shortcomings. Till twelfth, I used to be an incompetent student. The standard of education that children from rural areas get in government schools is appalling. They get neither the facilities nor the exposure to compete with urban kids from fancy English-medium schools. Despite facing hardships, I have come so far by the dint of my hard work and determination. The ground for comparison between two people shouldn't be merely their achievements. We should also take into account the circumstances in which they grew up, their surroundings and the resources they had at their disposal.'

While other members of the board nodded, Dr Mehta still remained unimpressed. 'These are excuses to cover up one's failures. Won't a boy, who fails in Maths and English, easily buckle under pressure in the administration? Anyway, let it be. Do you want to ask him any more questions?' he said to the other experts, without waiting for Manoj's response.

Another member asked, 'You are good at Hindi literature. Lectureship could be a good option for you. It's better to leave the job of running the district administration to those who have technological expertise. Only then will our country make progress.'

Literature now stood helplessly before technology. When English couldn't dent his confidence, technology was used as a weapon to unsettle him. Manoj thought for a while and then replied, 'Sir, you mean to say that a student of literature can't run a district. But our prime minister is a litterateur. Do you doubt his abilities too?' He gestured at the picture of Atal Bihari Vajpayee hanging on the wall. The alumnus of his MLB College Gwalior, the prime minster of India, became his shield.

The elderly member said excitedly, 'Excellent, Manoj!'

All the board members were impressed with his answer. Even Dr Mehta looked at him in stunned silence. He thought for a few seconds and then asked him to leave.

Manoj rose up to his feet, wished everyone a good day, and turned towards the door. At that moment, the elderly member, stopped him and asked, 'Which attempt is this?'

'Last attempt, sir,' Manoj answered.

'What will you do if you are not selected?'

'Swami Vivekananda's statement—"Arise, awake, and stop not till the goal is reached"—always inspires me. I'll also not stop till I achieve my goal,' Manoj answered, recalling his days spent at Vivekananda Kendra.

'What's your aim? Isn't it to become an IAS or an IPS officer?' The expert was a bit surprised by his answer.

'Becoming an IAS–IPS officer, a teacher or a librarian can't be the aim of one's life; it shouldn't be. These are only means to achieve a larger goal, which is to serve one's country with the utmost sincerity,' Manoj said.

His remarks were greeted by silence. With a gentle smile, the elderly man asked him to leave. Manoj wished them a pleasant day once again and stepped out of the room.

50

12 May—the day the final results were to be published. At 5 p.m., the names of successful candidates were to be displayed on the noticeboard of the UPSC office. All those who appear for the interview long to see their names on the list, but the bitter truth is that two-thirds of them are left out. Until the list comes out, everyone oscillates between hope and despair; no one is certain about success.

The clock struck four in the afternoon. Before setting off for the UPSC office, Manoj called up his father to get his blessings. 'Papa, final result will come out today,' he said.

'Oh, great. I want you to join the IPS.' His father had remained indifferent to all his results until now, but today he surprised Manoj with his enthusiasm. His words lifted Manoj's spirits. 'With your blessings, I'll definitely succeed.'

'Once you become an IPS officer, I'll not spare the deputy director. How dare he suspend me! I'll clip his wings, send him to jail. Then the bastard will realize what all the father of an IPS officer can do!' He dreamt of bringing his arch-enemy to his knees. Manoj couldn't help smiling at his naivety.

Accompanied by Shraddha, he reached the UPSC office in an autorickshaw. A throng of students and their well-wishers had already gathered on the road outside the gate. Both merged into the crowd. A constable was struggling to manage the traffic. He shoved Manoj aside and asked him to stand clear of the road. Manoj could feel his heart pounding as he reached the main gate.

The watchman chased everyone out and latched it from inside. After some five minutes, a member of the staff put up the result on the main noticeboard. Those five minutes felt like an age to Manoj. As soon as the gate was flung open, the crowd poured into the compound. On seeing the result, some students started dancing with joy, some broke down and cried, while some others slumped to the ground in despair. A few felt dizzy and nearly fainted.

Manoj couldn't gather the courage to see the result, so he sent Shraddha in instead and waited outside. Now everything depended on her yes or no. A group of students came out rocking with laughter followed by another lot with tear-streaked faces. One could see only these two categories of students today outside the UPSC building. Avinash came out with heavy steps, looking dejected. When Manoj asked him about his result, he just shook his head and walked away. Manoj felt even more nervous now. Some candidates walked past him saying that Hindi-medium candidates had fared miserably this year.

Feeling very tense, Manoj waited impatiently for Shraddha. At that instant, he spotted her walking towards him with a serious face. His heart sank; he guessed that she was going to break the bad news. 'What happened, Shraddha? Tell me,' he asked anxiously.

'Manoj,' she said, her voice low. She paused, and looked at his dazed expression. 'You've become an IPS officer!' she shouted.

He couldn't believe his ears. 'Say that again!'

Ecstatic, she repeated, 'You've become an IPS officer!'

Manoj still couldn't believe her. He asked, 'Are you sure you saw the correct roll number? Was my name there on the list? Or you did you see someone else's roll number!'

Shraddha had already verified both his roll number and name very carefully. She allayed his anxieties. Manoj heaved a euphoric sigh of relief. They got into an autorickshaw. The same constable who had shoved Manoj a few minutes ago was standing there. 'How was your result?' he asked curiously.

'IPS,' Manoj replied.

The cop gave him a salute immediately. Manoj looked at him in astonishment. In an instant, his success in an examination had changed the attitude of the world towards him. As he got down from the auto and hugged the constable, Manoj's eyes filled with tears. Never before in his life had the constable been embraced by an IPS officer. The autorickshaw moved towards Nehru Vihar. The wind combed through Manoj's long hair. Shraddha was ecstatic, tears had welled up in her eyes.

About the Author

Anurag Pathak is an Indore–based writer. He has previously published a collection of stories titled *WhatsApp Par Kranti* (Antika, 2016). Born in Gwalior on 5 August 1976, he holds a PhD in Hindi literature. He can be reached at 7869177525; authoranurag.p@gmail.com

About the Translators

Gautam Choubey teaches English at Atma Ram Sanatan Dharma College, University of Delhi. His English translation of Pandey Kapil's celebrated historical fiction *Phoolsunghi* (Penguin, 2020) is the first ever translation of a Bhojpuri novel. He has also translated Andre Béteille's *Democracy and its Institutions* (OUP, 2021) into Hindi. He tweets @GautamChoubey9 and can be reached at gautam.choubey922@gmail.com

Lalit Kumar teaches English at Deen Dayal Upadhyaya College, University of Delhi. His English translation of Harimohan Jha's classic Maithili novel *Kanyadan* will be published soon by Harper Perennial. He can be reached at manavlit85@gmail.com